T0149376

WALKING
MILES BY FAITH

MILDRED SPENCER

authorHOUSE®

AuthorHouse™
1663 Liberty Drive
Bloomington, IN 47403
www.authorhouse.com
Phone: 1 (800) 839-8640

Published by AuthorHouse 02/15/2019

ISBN: 978-1-5462-6968-7 (sc)
ISBN: 978-1-5462-6967-0 (e)

Print information available on the last page.

CONTENTS

ACKNOWLEDGEMENTS

It gives me great honor to acknowledge my three sons, one Spiritual Son; one Son-in law. My Spiritual mother, my two grandchildren, and two great grand babies! To my only Daughter-in-law for her ambition of introducing each family member in part. Also for expressing their love and apprehension to me in this book! "It is very humbling in my own personal life." Together all of us are "Walking Miles By Faith!" (2nd Corinthians 5:7) KJV: "For we walk by faith, not by sight." At times, most people subconsciously try to pull you back down to some "mediocrity" in which they departure.

I am thrilled, in revealing to the readers that there are some that have "True loved, honesty, and admiration" in my personal life! I have been fortunate enough to be surrounded by "strong women and men!" I have found out that, if you want something said, ask "A-Man!" If you want something done ask "A-woman!" But i am persuade by the Word of God, that says, "Again I say to you, if two of you agree on earth about anything they ask, it will be done for them by my Father in heaven" [Matthew 18:19].

I am sure many of you readers can recall a time in your life when the gifts of the Spirit operated through someone, that you can be "Re-energized by the Spirit of God." But in order for you to become a more yielded vessel so that the Holy Spirit can use you"? It was recently in my spirit, that I was thinking of the pressures and stress that affects so many people's lives; because they needed a place of worship that they can go to! I am also acknowledging conditions! That is how people live their lives in their 'cars' and spend endless hours on expressways each day. Mildred want to "acknowledge" you by letting you know; when you finally get home, you can't really rest. Why? Because, all, the bills must be paid; the children need special "ATTENTION" and "CHASTISEMENT!"

THEREFORE Walking through the door of the house at the end of the work day does not mean your work is finished. You have switched to a different kind of work. Then there are still church responsibilities. You want to be faithful to your church and serve in as many areas as possible. Yes, I did all of this in my home Church in "Los Angeles, CA." Church is important and should be treated as such.

Mildred wants to "Acknowledge every family"! There are family responsibilities. If you have an elderly person in your family, you know that this requires attention and energy too. Of course, you want to do this! This isn't an obligation: it is a privilege to take care of older family members. I can't get to "my Spiritual mother" like I want to, in "Palms Springs", however, I make sure she is doing ok! And if you live in an area where you are close to cousins, aunts, uncles, brothers, sisters, and grandparents, you must also work all these precious people into the schedule. Birthdays, anniversaries, funeral's weddings all of these are part of our family responsibilities that require your time, energy, and finances.

Mildred wants to acknowledge "your friendship responsibilities". Friendships require time and attention. As a good friend, you want to be there for your friend's good times and bad times. You probably believe that you should be available when they need to talk about a problem. You want to spend time with your friends because you need to enjoy their fellowship. But all this requires time and energy as well. One of Satan's greatest weapons is discouragement, and he knows exactly when to use it. He waits until you are tired weak, and susceptible to his lies. Then he hits you hard in your emotions, trying to tell you that you are accomplishing nothing valuable in life. Friends of mine across this world. In those moments when Mildred feel physically exhausted and yet I see no pause in my schedule, I turn to "Romans 8:11", for encouragement. It says, "But if the Spirit of him that raised up Jesus from the dead dwell in you, he that raised up Christ from the dead shall also quicken your mortal bodies by his Spirit that dwelleth in you. This means that if you will yield to the Holy Spirit who dwells in you He will supernaturally revitalize you. He will rejuvenate you. He will refresh you with a brand-new surge of supernatural life. He will fill you with so much resurrection power that you will be ready to get up and go again! May I leave this prayer of "acknowledge" for you day by day!

"Lord, to release the resurrection power of Jesus Christ that resides in my Spirit. Let it flow up into my body and mind so I can be rejuvenated, and be recharged with enough power to fulfill all responsibilities and duties that comes before me. I pray this in Jesus' name!

ACKNOWLEDGEMENTS OF: "PERSONS WITH ADMIRATIONS IN MY LIFE TIME:"

- Nieces/Bessy, at the "Navy Base," In Sacramento, CA.
- Elder Bob Carrol, "A musician: "[many times, plays for me in revivals]" !
- Apostle Ruby Johnson, Flint Mich. [Thank you for heaving me [six years] !
- Bishop B. Jefferson, Flint Mich. [Thank you for having me for (four years]!
- My Sister, 1st Lady Connie, and Husband-Bishop R. Deloatch!
- Dr. Mattie Cook. [Preached, for my deceased daughter, many times] !
- My God given Sister/ Brother; Brenda/Clayton; NV. [Thanks for your love] !
- Missy. Frankie/Deacon Benny Williams. [Thanks for who you are]!
- Bro. Eddie/wife Katrina she sung at my "[eighty birthday celebration] !"

A special acknowledgement to: Mary Ellen-Willams., "A saved nurse, "who cared for me, after returning for the "emergency room" in [2018]. Thank you for your support, and for being so caring and so kind! You and your "young son" treated me like a "princess," and [YOU] treated me like a woman "longs to be treated"! Love, to all your sons! "Myles, Montel and Maxwell!

"Jacqueline R. Stoot," Executive Assistant/ "A Paralegal"

"MY INTERNATIONAL ADJUTANT" Nicole;" request by my daughter, to have Nicole Licensed at her "funeral Procession," Eulogized by her Spiritual Son "Supt. A. Powers" in (2011)

MY LOCAL ADJUTANT" Evang. Vicki;" was led by the "Word of God,

FOREWORD

I was pleasantly asked to submit a few brief words in the Forward of Dr. Evangelist Mildred Spencer, my mother-in-law' new book. I am fortunate to have been considered to have a special place in Dr. Spencer's heart.

Dr. Evangelist Mildred B. Spencer is truly a phenomenal mother, wife, mentor and virtuous woman of God. For over sixty years she has preached and taught people of all ages, races, and faiths about the goodness of God and has done so globally. She has made this her life's work and there are many whose lives have been changed forever because of her teachings. In addition to being a highly respected evangelist, Dr. Spencer has also counseled many people, including couples and families. Going further she is also a former teacher and has that teaching a mentoring spirit by nature.

Dr. Spencer is the matriarch of her family and raised four children along with her husband Nathanial L. Spencer Sr. Together they instilled core values such as working hard, family loyalty and putting God first. Dr. Spencer continues to be the guiding light in her immediate and extended families. Her nurturing has created an unbreakable family bond. Additionally, she is the spiritual mother to many who have crossed her path. Dr. Spencer has the ability to put others at ease with her warm smile, infectious laugh and sense of humor, that only individuals close to her really have an opportunity to see.

Faith plays a critical element in our lives and to this end, I want to send the warmest love and congratulations for completing another compelling new book, "Walking Miles By Faith".

Ephesians 2:8-9 ESV

For by grace you have been saved through faith. And this is not your own doing; it is the gift of God, not a result of works, so that no one may boast.

Denise K. Spencer MHS

I am the elder son of my mother, Dr. Evangelist Mildred B. Spencer.

Behind every great man is his mother. Someone imagined the mother of three son:

Having a sincere faith doesn't imply perfection. But it does imply reality with God. Such faith dwelt in my mother; it was at home in with her, a comfortable, everyday sort of thing.

Sincere faith means that you have sincerely believed in Jesus Christ as your savior and Lord. It means that you walk in reality with Christ each day, spending time in his World and in prayer. It means that you confront yourself with Scripture and Judge your sin on the thought level. It means that when you do sin against a family member, you ask their forgiveness and seek to work on your weak areas. It means that you develop godly character qualities and attitudes of submission, thankfulness, and joy of the Lord. I realize that, while mom isn't perfect, she does walk with God.

THANK YOU FOR YOUR UNCONDITIONAL LOVE AND FRIENDSHIP;

I remembered being the oldest son, when my mother took

time out to tell us how to respect young lady friends, so that her mother would not be disappointed from a young man. I also can remembered the time when I was preparing to go to my “Senior Prom”, I was so excited until I made a mistake and had two limousines showed up at the same time at the house. That was an exciting moment for my mother and my late father. My mother was very careful of how my brothers and I dressed and looked.

THANK YOU FOR ALWAYS BELIEVING IN ME;

Life has been difficult and there have been times when I’ve felt like giving up, when things were not going my way. Each time, my mother was there to remind me of my worth as a human being.

My mother has encourage me to keep reaching for the unreachable and never settle for anything less than I deserved. No matter how bizarre my dreams were — from astronaut or just being a hard worker— my mother always told me to go after what would make me happy.

As life goes on, I realize more and more how much you have done for me and continue to do every day.

As a grown man, with my own business, I always make sure that my mother is well taken care of.

-Nathaniel Levi Spencer, Jr., elder son
Irvine, CA

It is with great delight that I am able to share a few words of dedication and appreciation for my mother Dr. Evangelist Mildred Betty Spencer. At an early age, I understood the meaning of strength, family, dedication, loyalty, and faith. Dr. Spencer has been preaching the gospel longer than all of my siblings have been alive and I truly feel that she has been touched by the un-wielding hand of the spirit to share her divine wisdom and love.

Dr. Spencer has separated herself from her peers by simply being true to herself and the word she holds dear; what she says is what she does. Through the many years of traveling and serving the Lord, she has had an uncanny mannerism of reflecting a positive attitude when times may have been tough.

The appreciation of her sacrifices at times, may have appeared to be lacking although, she handled it with grace. Our family has watched her labor in ministry after sixty years of putting in work has gradually affected her body, although she remains just as sprite as she ever has. I adore my mother, respect her for whom she is. Dr. Spencer has multi-tasked in being a mother, wife, grandmother, counselor, educator, evangelist and more than anything else an exceptional lady in Christ.

Dr. Spencer encompasses compassion and a generosity that is unequal. One of the greatest moments was the opportunity to have my mother flown out to Montego Bay, Jamaica to be a part of my wife and l, destination wedding a feat we will never forget as she flew for almost forty-eight hours of traveling from preaching in different locations in the United States. Dr. Spencer has graciously spread the word in various location in the world from Europe, Great Britain, Germany, France, Hawaii, and countless location in the United States.

There has been a great many people whom you have opened our home too, churches you have led, people you have counseled and even during the times you may have felt unappreciated; you were always dignified in your actions. Wisdom always prevailed. There are talented preachers' in the world now, but few could compare to the raw passion and the delivery of your messages on the pulpit. We are all so blessed to have you as our matriarch and extremely proud to call you mom. Congratulations on your continued accomplishments and authoring another fantastic book. I Love you dearly mom.

Proverbs 31:25-30

Strength and dignity are her clothing, and she laughs at the time to come. She opens her mouth with wisdom, and the teaching of kindness is on her tongue. She looks well to the ways of her household and does not eat the bread of idleness. Her children rise up and call her blessed; her husband also, and he praises her: "Many women.have done excellently, but you surpass them all.

Gerald T Spencer M.B.A.

I am Terrance J. Spencer. The middle son of three. Brothers to Nathaniel and Gerald Spencer and a child of four. Rest in peace Debra Richardson, my one and only sister. She was one of the biggest blessings in my life.

It is with my utmost gracious pleasure to applaud and congratulate Dr. Evangelist Mildred B. Spencer in her many successful attempts to accomplish specific projects. Dr. Spencer has exemplified a fierce tenacity in serving for Christ as an amazingly strong, selfless, loyal and loving mother.

Dr. Spencer has made such a big impact in the lives of so many people locally, nationally as well as internationally. She has always supplied more than plenty. Plenty of food, safety, security, shelter and love. No one can take your place, although you take the place of so many others.

I feel so very Blessed to have Dr. Spencer as my Angel, friend and mother. Honored to witness your intricate blend of gentility and toughness. She taught me to never back down and fight for everything I believe. Thank you for the things you felt obligated and didn't have to do for me. I remember coming from Boston, MA to Inglewood California in 1973 and you where my 6th grade substitute teacher at Jefferson Elementary. You treated me equal and fair to my classmates.

Thank you, mom, for being my strength I always needed while learning to fly, even though you sometimes had to catch me when I fall. I soar higher now because of you. Thank you for teaching me the importance of hard work. I just wish, I taught you, not to cheer for the opposing football team while sitting in the home field seats.

My sincerest praise and purest of love.
You are my HERO!

Terrance Spencer

FOREWORD

A very good friend invited me to a church revival with the intentions of introducing me to a young lady. While in service I actually befriended the revivalist. Unbeknownst to me, the revivalist was actually the young lady's mother!

Imagine, being prayed for and anointed by mother of the girl you wanted to date, prior to being introduced. Needless to say, I married her daughter. This has been the essence of my relationship with Evangelist Mildred Spencer.

Unlike, so many of the horror stories one may hear about the dreaded in-laws, our relationship has been based on love, respect, honor, and plenty of laughs.

I believe what inspires me the most about Dr. Spencer, is her sincere devotions to God. Many times, particularly at night, I would sit at the foot of the stairs and listen to her praying and praising God all by herself in her room. My first encounter of this was my first sleep-over at the house, and being awaken at one o'clock in the morning by shouts of hallelujah and glory!

From this experience, I encourage as many as I can to develop their own personal devotion to God. Every message she preaches is filled with power, love, and conviction, whether it is with a congregation of five or five hundred!

With touches of her personal experiences, which demonstrates that if God could do it for her, God can do it for you. I believe everyone who reads this book will understand how anyone who trusts God can literally "Walk Miles by Faith"! It is my honor to produce these words to encourage you, the reader, as well as to bear witness of my mother-in-law, Dr. Mildred Spencer.

The Rose of Sharon Evangelistic COGIC, Moreno Valley, Ca,

Pastor, Leodis Richardson Jr.

In celebration of Evangelist Dr. Mildred Spencer's new book "Walking Miles by Faith". It caused me to reflect back to August 2010, and little did I know that God was birthing something very profound, I was trying to adjust to life without my natural Mother, who at this time had transitioned on to be the Lord.

During our 11th year Holy Convocation which was held at Victory Temple of Deliverance Ministry in Moreno Valley, California. This small in stature, powerhouse of a woman had came in to share a Word with us, while sharing God began to speak to me, regarding this Woman of God, becoming my Spiritual Mother, as if to say "Son Behold your Mother". Afterwards I shared with her what God had spoken into my spirit; and she affirmed that it also had begun to resonate into her spirit as well.

From that day to this, I have been acknowledged as her eldest son amongst my three brothers. To confirm that this position had been the Will of God, during my recovery from my second cancer surgery, (which today, I might add, I am Cancer Free).

While praying and attending to my physical and spiritual needs, my two sisters Thomasena Simmons, and Shelia Yvette

Johnson began to see and encounter the spirit of a Mother within her. Additionally, they began to yearn for her to cover them. In early 2017 she adopted them as her daughters covering them as well.

To know this Woman is to know she is a confidant, a counselor, and a warrior who fights on your behalf. I have witnessed in part her amazing journey and found it be fitting to this title, "Walking Her Miles By Faith", she can attest to the many miracles God has performed in her life, just as equally as she can attest of the many miracles that He has performed for His people using her as His extended Hand.

I would suggest that you sit back, reclined your mind, and partake of this book which will cause your Faith to arise as you walk through this written work which allows you to see and feel the many "Miles Walked by Faith".

Foreword by: Bishop Randy D. Triplett, Sr. Pastor

Victory Temple of Deliverance Ministries

Moreno Valley, California

PREFACE

AUTHOR HISTORY

My name is, Mildred B. Spencer. I am an 'African American' female! I was born in South Carolina. And I was told, at the age of [2-yearsl, that one of my mother's friend, 'twelve-year-old son' was watching me while they were "Picking Cotton," across the road side. It was told, my mother had me sitting in a little wooden rocking chair, near the fire place, because, the weather was cool! But suddenly, they saw the "boy dragging 'ME' out into the yard with "flames of fire burning!"

As I grew older, I understood that my mother had passed away! Therefore, my Father, A pastor, and the "Apostolic mother" from the church that raised me; they began to tell me the story of my young life; and why this "BURN SPOT REMAINS ON THE RIGHT SIDE OF MY FACE"! They told me, that the boy said; he did not intend to; 'burn me'. He said, he took a straw from the homemade broom and stuck it into the fire place. Then he lit my dress, but he did not intent for it to burn that fast! However, I was told, everybody ran from the cotton field, to put the flame out!

My father said, the doctors came with their "equipment's."

And after the examination, they rapped my entirely body; except my "eyes, nose, mouth" Then the doctors told them, "if I recover, I would be like a vegetable," simply because of swallowing so much smoke! Plus, I might be "no taller then (3-feet) tall! After which, they took me to the church twice a day to pray and anointed my eyes, mouth, and nose! Thank God for such anointing at that time! They said, there was a great "Miraculously healing by the Hands of God!" "Doctors Treat, God Heals."

Friends: because of my healing, I am "Walking Miles by Faith!" Now, I have graduated from "Russellville High School" in South Carolina, with a [four-years] scholarship! Therefore, I was sent to collage in "Boston Massachusetts." My Studies consist of; Cosmetologist, "Child-care Development," sewing and, Home Economics!" The theme of it all is, [A PLACE FOR EVERYTHING AND EVERYTHING IN IT'S PLACE]!

Again, I'm "Walking Miles By Faith," I started singing with the "Biblical:" along with [now] "Bishop Sims," and musician Helen! As I got older, I got married!

In the meantime; I was (called to Ministry, at the age of seventeen)! "I realized that the Holy Spirit was moving in my Spirit about "being called!" So, I obeyed the voice of God! Therefore; I could not sing anymore! And by the way, this was a very scary time for me in my life! So now, with all the Praying and of course, inquiring how to develop sermons! The message got out to "Pastor Barrow." He took me with his only daughter "Claudia He taught "Bible college in his home." Of course, I learned a lot! However: I really did not start preaching until I was [age-nineteen]! The places are located: in New York, Connecticut and a few more!

One night, I was half asleep when I had a "Vision!" I never knew what a vision was! But I absolutely saw my self-standing in a well-known "pastor's pulpit." And, I was dressed in a "white nurses' uniform." Then I heard a voice on my right side.

When I looked, I saw a "White Cup" over my shoulder. The "Voice said" take this "CUP," and hold it over the people's head! People of God, I saw myself, stepping down; while walking into a small isle; holding this "CUP over the peoples heads,"

When I got to the back of the church, I saw the back petition disappeared! I kept walking with that "CUP of SALVATION" in my hand! As far as I could see, it looked like a "Sea of people!" When I finally woke up a little, I was so surprise!" shaking! When I came to full circle of where I was now, in my bed! I began to cry out to the Lord, and in my spirit, I heard these words, your position is: "Fieldwork for God! "This is your calling!"

At about that time, our three "Covenant sisters," were new in ministry! [Marie, Helen and Il, speaking in Boston. But I was still "Walking Miles by Faith," focusing, how to prepare messages! "In the meanwhile, I received a "Telegram from my father "Pastor Alvin Edwards", [which is my maiden name]. It was an invitation for me to come home and speak at his church in, 'South Carolina'. I had no children at that time! Also, my husband was on the "campaign Trail" in [1959]. When I spoke to my husband about the trip, and of course, he did not want me to travel alone. However, he knew how good of a 'house keeper Miss Shirly was', Therefore, he asked her to travel along with his wife! She agreed, and he paid for her and two of her young daughters to take the trip!

When I arrived home, my father was blessed to have his daughter especially, after all he witness in my life as a child, and now, I am about to "speak at his church!" My text was taken from [Psalms Chapter 1:3] Two months after I returned home in Boston, I received another "Telegram saying that my father had passed away"! Now, there is not a family member left in my life! But by the Grace of God, I keep 'Walking Miles By Faith!' Furthermore, I was already "Licensed in 'Toledo Ohio;' but now here I am in other services there; "One of the messages given to me by the Holy spirit; was: "WHAT ARE YOU GOING TO DO, WHEN THE WORLD'S ON FIRE?" This was history in my life time! After the message was just about finished, the "Firemen, open the door, because the city was on fire! They made the announcement, that people were throwing [TORCHE'S], in building! Thank God, "the Church was Saved!" At another time, my covenant sister, Helen wakens, and I was "Ordained in the convention."

After returning home, "Bishop Foxworth" in my home town asked me to conduct a week's revival for his church! A "Military family was visiting their parents, at the church! Sister Shirly knew the young lady [Nadine] and her husband. After service, they greeted me, and asked for my information! in [1969] I received a "certified letter" of invitation from the "commanding Chief;" asking if I could come and Minister at the "Military Base!" I was the 'First Female Evangelist" to speak in 'Frankfurt Germany," at the military base! Traveling along with me was, my [1 year old], 'Gerald Spencer,' why?

Because he was not taking bottles yet! Those militaries treated me with great admiration! For instant, the Base provided nurses, to care for my baby most of the time!

The Bible emphasizes that Faith is a gift because God deserves all the 'Glory for our Salvation' [Eph.2:9].That's why I am blessed to be "Walking Miles by Faith!" My husband and I went to visit his parents in "North Carolina". Across from them, was a very close neighbor included, 'Shirley Caesar' that lived there as well. When I was introduced to her, 'Shirley Ceaser', asked me to be the (MC), for her Consert in '"Rhode Island, Connecticut? I said yet! Several cars drown along with us. After the Consert, A 'Lady Pastor' invited me to speak at her church in the city. It was "A Salvation Army Church." So, It was my responsibility because, 'Field Work' doesn't have any singular "Denomination."

Even though I was young in age, I was still leaving! But what I knew at that time was based on a 'solid foundation'! "[l believed in what I was called to do]! "Go ye into all the world, and preach the "Gospel to every creature" [Mark 16:15]. This Word is speaking to me personal! It is not about denomination; even though I am filled with the "Holy Ghost and fire," my responability is about Souls! The Holy Spirit will lead and guide me how to conduct myself in any given service! I must announce that', "Souls were saved, Sister Shirly Jones rode in one of the cars, to church and her oldest daughter, received the "Holy Ghost" in a "Salvation Army Church!" She is now an "Evangelist" in another place! Furthermore, it was a time of identifying wigs after service for the ladies! (Psalm 118:23-24)), "This is the LORD's doing: it is marvelous in our eyes!" Thank God I am still, "Walking Miles by Faith!"

Readers, there is nothing too hard for God to do, if we trust and believe in the work that God has appointed us to do; I promise you, "you will succeed in it!" To all the people that have been called of God to do 'His work on the Field', and to work otherwise, I am praying for you as well, that you will always be in the will of God! After I return home to Boston, I was asked by my [use to be teacher] "Pastor Barrow" who taught me at his home 'Bible collage', to speak at his convention, also his daughter! There were 'Delegates' from different countries! After the convention, please note: in [Acts 20: 28-20], says, the Holy Spirit made you Oversees [Bishop],. Therefore, one of the Overseers from "[Brixton England]" invited me to come and Minister at his 'Place of Worship'. The Lord allowed me to travel [twenty two times], to minster for other Overseers and pastors as well. Prayer is the Answer when we Walk by Faith!

In the year of [1972], we moved to California, because my husband was transferred. At that time, we participated in church work where "My husband's two sisters and mother attended! It was the "Greater Page Temple COGIC," with the "Presiding Bishop Page," and "First lady Page!" Bishop Page, asked me to do several revivals there!" At one revival, it was near the ending, that 'Bishop Page', told the "administrative staff" of which, one was, my husband's sister "Lillian Snowden: to order, a CAPE for "Evangelist [Hatchet]! I quote: Bishop Page said to the congregation: I am calling her [Evangelist Hatchet], because how she "Cut's the Word of God into the minds of God's people"! During that particular service, our nephew, 'Gregory Snowden' was Filled with the Holy Ghost! Also, our [deceased daughter Debra], was filled the same time;

at age 12! She said to her father, [Daddy, I couldn't stop my shoes from moving]! Therefore, I MUST give God [All the glory], for what He has done for His people!

It was the last night of the revival, that 'Bishop Anointed the "Cape," and placed it on "ME!" I am yet giving God all the praise and thanks for "HIS ANOINTING!" A few years after that, "Bishop passed away, at the age of [100 plus]! Over 70 years, the two sisters are still at "Page Temple Church!" also, my nephew [Gregory Snowden] now a retired officer!

I am still "Walking Miles by Faith!" In [1976], My husband and I was led to join "Tower of Faith Pentecostal Church", which is now, "COGIC!" under the leadership of, "Dr. pastor, Rueben Paul Anderson, and First Lady Anderson!" My position was the "youth Director." At the beginning, we started with [nine youth], including my four children, and the Pastor's two children. Shortly, we were into the hundreds! In the meantime, I was still traveling part time on the field. In between we were working on many projects for all youth! Also, we had several "King and Queen pageants," of different ages! After the pageants, here are some of the places, they went! "I took the courts" along with some of the leaders, to places like: "Hawaii, and "San Francisco, CA."

As I began "Walking Miles by Faith," In [19931, I completed "Christian Ethics,"

Local Church Administration, and Christian Counseling," A home study from the University of Biblical Studies, Bethany, Oklahoma!" Within that same year, I was thankful to God; after traveling to "Jamaica" for many years, to have my "pastor Anderson," and fifteen other members to travel along with me to Jamaica, in support for me! The time was right! Why?

Because this was the very first time, "an American Hotel was built in Jamaica!" Not only that, because they blessed me by giving their support, God Himself showed 'FAVOR' to my Pastor!" After we left, so many Pastors, officers and members traveled to the [USA] to become a part of my pastor's Ministry! When God's power takes over your life, nothing is impossible!

I must keep 'WORKING!' for the Master! "Walking Miles By Faith!" I had the most honest and loving husband in Jesus's Name! He was so concern about me having to learn more about Ministry! Why? Because, in my travels, [his words], 'I do not want you to be intimidated by anyone, especially men!" Therefore, he enrolled me for night classes at the "California Baptist College" in Riverside, California. My husband paid all the 'tuition fees' that was needed for the years, I would attend!

Then, I only traveled on weekends; because of my studies! After finishing two courses: I traveled back to "Bermuda for the third time, for just three days! After I return home, 'TRAGEDY CAME MY WAY!" After a few days, my husband was not feeling well! Of Course, prayer was going up for him! His doctor insist that he go to the hospital! All my sons were young adults, only two were away from home in university's! My daughter who was an [RN], drove us to the hospital in Riverside! After being in the room for a few hours, he said to me "honey," go home and rest! I am sure many of you have experience 'tragedy as well!' But God! I am not alone! As soon as I got home, I received a call that he was in the "intensive care units!"

I return to the hospital, and never left! Why? because of his position being a "secret-service" with the government, I was taken care of very well! Now my husband is in a coma! I was watching all the lights flashing! Of course he has a 'niece' that is a doctor, flew in. both her and my daughter Debra, a [RN], cared for him along with the main doctors! The Red Cross" send for my Son-law, a "Military in Japan," to come to the hospital! I am sure many of you in this world, have had some tragic things happen in your lives! Therefore, you can attest to what I am saying!

So, the doctor's suggestion was given, maybe, if your husband hears a [formula voice] he might just wake up! I thought about my 'grand baby; "Chimel Stacy," almost two years old! She was her granddad's heart! My daughter brought her in! When the doctor took her over to the head of the bed, SHE YELLED OUT, GRANDDADDY? My husband immediately opens his eyes! But, friends, he closed his eyes and never open again! Here is a word for all of you that are reading this book! Stay committed! (2 nd Timothy 4:7) says," I have fought a good fight" I have finished my course, I have kept the faith! "Remember the good days!" As I was lying on the little bed they put in the intensive room for me. I heard the Holy Spirit saying, write the "Obituary!"

I had two sons' in collage away from home. And they came home to be with their father, at 'his bedside! The oldest son, had a business that his father, had a hand in it for him! My husband passed away (3-minutes) after midnight, right into Mother's Day! To all the "mothers," Be faithful to God, and you will be blessed!" My middle age son was expecting his 'Dad' to be at his graduation the next month at the "Sonoma State University!

However, many of you mothers are thinking just like I did!

It is vital to be supportive to your children! For that cause, I had to talk to "(Dr. Tervis C. Deen) at the collage, letting him know I can not finish my classes, for the reason of my husband's death! In the meantime, I was led to write a book about "What affects A Widow?" I continued being faithful, doing God's work. The Bible speaks of many miracles; that shows God's power and helps us to believe in Him! [Jeremiah 32:27]! For I am the Lord, the God of all people. Nothing is too difficult for me!" Readers, that's why, I can keep on "Walking by faith!"

One afternoon I was studying for a service I had to go to. And my little grand daughter Chimel, came up stairs to my room, and said Grandma, look at how I am drawing this picture for you! Right then the phone ringed! It was the "Dean of another university!" She wanted to know my name. Then she said someone told her about me from another collage; and said due to the death of your husband, you had to leave the collage that you were attending! Believer me, 'God knows our Faith!" To make it short, God allowed me to attend the "Practical Christianity Institute of Evangelism." I am yet praising God for allowing me to graduate with honors at the age of [73] years old, with a "Doctoral Theology Degree."

At that graduation, it was joy to see almost [200] guests: as well as all of my children along with my future "Daughter-in-law" at that time! Some were "Pastors, Apostles, from different states, staying in hotels just to see me walk!

Also, I was graduated with honor! Thank you, God, for: "Walking Miles By Faith!"

Shortly after my husband passed, I received an invitation to Minister at "Pastor Pearson's Church in "San Diego CA," he was the nephew of [Mother Pearson] in Oklahoma City! While we were there, he called his Uncle "Carlton Parson" in Oklahoma and told him about me! After I left to come home, Shortly I received a call inviting me to speak for "Mother Pearson's women's service in their convention held at "Oral Roberts university." With thousands of people! Traveling along with me was, "Sister Sweet' a prayer warrior from "Faith Temple Church" in Riverside CA. "Pastor Sims"! At that time, It was the same time, that the Holy Spirit, moved on my heart to write a book about my life and my husband!

Therefore, I traveled with my scrips, that was written already for my book; just in case the Lord gives me something more to write if need be.

Friends, I knew nothing about having a book published! While dinner was being served to all the guest, Pastors, and Evangelist. Also, Leaders from far and near were in that room! The "host pastor was greetings each one of us at our tables! When He came to the table where I was, the conversation continued! At that time, He said to me, I remember them saying, in the sanctuary, that you are a "Recent Widower." As we are talking, I said yes. And I am 'writing a book'. He said to me, what is "The title of the book"? I told him "What Affects A Widow," however, I need to find a publisher because I am almost finished with the book!

This 'Host Pastor' took it upon himself and said, do you mind if I have your number? And here is my phone number, as well as my wife's number! Then he stood back, and said to me, "I feel the Spirit of the Lord leading me to have my publisher that I worked with for years at my church here in the city to publish your book without any cost! He said, furthermore, for you to preach like you did, and just lost your husband, God has to bless you'"! And you will be blessed! Readers, from that time until now, door's have been open until, I can hardly fulfill all of them! My live will always be humble in Jesus's Name!" "Profiles of Faith"!

James the Half Brother of Jesus, taught about faith, telling us that true faith is demonstrated by what we are, how we live and what we do. [John 7:51] Yes doors never stopped opening! While I was there at "Oral Roberts University" in the convention, two lady Pastors came to me out side, and began to talk, They received my card! Shortly afterward, I was invited to "Flint Michigan." For 'Pastor Bernadel Jefferson, [now she is] 'Bishop Bernadel Jeffeson" and we are truly sisters in the Lord! It was an honor to serve [four years] preaching the Word of God! Also to be there for her "Consecration of Bishop' The same for the second lady pastor along with her. [Now she is] "Apostle Ruby Johnson," I spoke at her church about [six years], also in flint, Michigan. She is an anointed woman of God!

Lastly, in 2007- I was advanced to the "Pacific Coast" in areas of Seattle,

Tacoma and Spokane, WA. For "Pastor Jones" I am greatful for the "Bomon's! "Walking Miles By Faith" is all about =This Author' Dr. Mildred B. Spencer"

Out of all the women in the world, you choose me to be your Mother many years ago. What a joy you have been to me and my family, Mary Alice, Merchell, Angela, Donyale, Arnold, Javon, Tevin and Jimmae. You have prayed for us, you have loved us, you have encouraged us and you have blessed us. There are times when I need an uplifting word and my phone would ring and it was you, for that I'm so thankful. I pray God continue to strengthen and anoint you for the work He have called you to do. Stay dress with the whole armor of God and remember what Paul said in Philippians 4:13 "I can do all things through Christ which strengtheneth me."

We LOVE you and congratulations on your new book,
Your Chosen Mother,

Jimmie M. Giles

WHO AM I?

"First Lady Debra Spencer. Richardson"

The deceased daughter of "Dr. Evangelist Mildred Spencer.

The role of women in family, society, and church has been one of the most hotly debated issues in the history of the Christian church. Perhaps more important than the issue of a woman's place is the foundational question underlying the issue: "Who is woman?" or "What does it mean to be a woman? They were praising Mary, the mother of Jesus, and Debra, the "Queen of Heaven; that's where WE ARE!"

"Debra's" mouth was filled with laughter, and her tongue with singing (Psalm 126:2), because she loves her: "CHURCH SISTERS," for eighteen years; before she went to HEAVEN !

- Dr. Evette Denton
- Evangelist, Angela Warren
- District Missionary: Hidie Newton
- Evangelist, Vickie Jackson

- Evangelist, Linda Greer
- Pastor Edith Rogers; "1st lady Debra's sister" expressing her gratitude for opening her home for their ministry. Debra will never forget the highest appreciation for her.

Deceased — Daughter', 1st Lady Debra, and mother,

Dr. Evangelist Mildred B. Spencer

“And if you faithfully obey the voice of the Lord your God, being careful to do all his commandments that I command you today, the Lord your God Will set you high above all the nations of the earth. And all these blessings shall come upon you and overtake you, If you obey the voice of the Lord your God. Blessed shall you be In the City and blessed shall you be in the field. Blessed shall be the fruit of your womb and the fruit of your ground and the fruit of your cattle, the increase of your herds and the young of your flock Blessed shall be your basket and your kneading bowl.

Deuteronomy 28:1-68

Dr. Evangelist Mildred Spencer

CHAPTER 1

"DOCTORS TREAT." "GOD HEALS."

When you go to a "doctor", you may not like what the doctor says to you, but it's good for you! For an example, when I preach: some may not like what I am saying about your "Walk" with God, but if you would believe the message sent by God, I promise it will bless you in many ways! That's why Doctors are great, aren't they? We trust doctors when our child gets sick, our mothers gets sick, or even when we get sick. We trust that the Doctor can prescribe something to make us fell better. But, what happens when they give us the news that the sickness we are dealing with is beyond the work of their hands? Do we cruble saying it is hopeless or do we prevail saying, "l know my doctor knows his/her stuff, but thankfully, I know the Great Physician who created my body to function. I know the Creator who forms the human body effortlessly repeatedly! This is why I am saying: "Doctor's Treat" but "God Heals." lf only we could grasp this fact for real. It seems a lot of us are guilty of putting all of our trust and hopes in what the Doctor says. You see, science says that the condition is permanent, or science may not have a cure for that sickness or disease.

You see, I am a bit believer in the "Doctrine of Healing," You will see that I have experienced God's healing in my own life, and have witnessed God healing Countless people over the years I've been in Ministry, I am greatly comforted by verses like the one in James that gives us a great hope in the "Power of Prayer." As you read this book, you will see how I was "Hit with a condition, in the year of (2010); while my daughter was alive. The condition was called "PSORIASIS". I was tormented with pain for years, while yet "Ministering." Jesus didn't just die on the cross for your sins, He died on the cross for our sins, sickness, disease, and wounds. The healing is already ours, all we must do is believe it, seek it, and declare it. Don't be defeated by mere words: The devil wants you to think that what you are dealing with it permanently or incurable. The devil wants you to think you are already defeated, He doesn't want you to realize that Jesus already took care of that sickness, disease, or condition for you., Don't get me wrong, We are "Walking Milles By Faith." I was 'tired and tempted' for "seven years," going miles to see the doctor...But I never stopped. My assignment was very important. That's why when I entered "the house of God." I walk in with praise! I do not see Any One, but Jesus my, "healer and Redeemer."

The mystery we need to understand is this; at what point did the devil think he win's? At what point did people start believing that healing wasn't theirs?

Therefore, did these specific diagnoses become "permanent"? The Bible said, "Jesus is the same yesterday today and forever." So, Jesus is telling me, what He did for the man with leprosy, and the woman with the blood issuers, also, what He did for the lame, He can do for anybody! After reading [Acts ch.5: '15].

I was blessed by the Word that was told; It is of great importance that we bear in mind that while the gospel of Christ calls us into personal relationship with Him, it is a relationship which nevertheless has social consequences. We must remember that while His blessing begins with us it by no means ends with us for 'no man lives unto himself.' We must recognize that while we are units in the Kingdom of God, we are nevertheless joined to an in-numerable company of similar units, and that our influence is forever spreading, just as leaven spreads in a lump. Healing is ours! You don't have to live like that now, because He owns full restoration. What the devil stole from him, he must return! Praise God for gentle, powerful, compassionate God! Doctors are awesome, but just remember what science tells us does not line up with the Word, let's choose to believe and Trust in God. After all, we place our whole lives in his hands! "Doctors Treat." God Heals." Right after that condition, another illness was taken place within my "Vocal-Cord." Because of that, I had "Nerve damage," and of course, it caused hoarseness, a reduction in speech volume, also pain in the throat when speaking or Preaching! I was told by the 'doctor, not to preach.' I must say; I believe in doctors as will as respecting them. But because "God called me", by Faith I believed the Word of God, that says God who works in you both to will and to work, for his good pleasure, [Philippians 2:13], however, I used wisdom. So, I continued to preach by "Speaking Softly!" Even though the doctor told me not to Preach!" yet, obeying the Voice of God, that said" I called you to preach my Word." It didn't matter what people would say or think, about me speaking soft; I remained in the will of God!

I remembered, there were times I had to go to my doctor, to have my "VocalCord" examine! But friends of mine, at this time, the doctor did an examination and 'he himself was amazed', because he could not find any more [nerve damages or build up fluids]! "God Heals!" I received a "New Vocal-Cord," and full restoration! What the devil though he "stole from me, God returned back to me a New Vocal-Cord!" I must give Him praise for a gentle, powerful, compassionate God! Therefore, on the surface, the question of weather Christians should go to doctors, is some what ridiculous! Because "Luke was a physician" Many hospitals were started by Churches! There is nothing in the Bible that forbids a believer from seeing a physician. I personally thank God for the surgeons! Know body wants unnecessary surgery. However, God can help you recover from surgery!

God can work "Miracles through doctors." Its bout your Faith! And the Lord said, if you have faith as a grain of mustard seed, ye might say unto this sycamore tree, be plucked up by the root, and be thou planted in the sea: an it shall obey you, [Lk. 17:61] In the year of 2001, I had a "Total Knee replacement," on my "Right Knee." Doctors Treat", therefore, I must give the surgeon praise! But God did the Healing! I was right back on the "Mission Field!" now in [2003], I had a 'Torn Rotator Cuff Repair" on my left arm! I was still "Walking by Faith", I received another "Healing from God!" I was back on the Mission Field again! As times went on, in [2006], I had an "Orthopedic Surgery" on my "Left Arm!" God is a Healer!

Once again in the year of [2011], right after "my only daughter passed away," I had another, "Total Knee Replacement," on my Left knee! Thank God for Healings! I was right back on the "Mission Field!" I felt the need to write about what seems impossible, to man, is possible with God! He is the HEALER!

My total life is in the hands of our "Lord and Savior Jesus Christ!" it was this year in [2018], I heard the 'Spirit of God", calling me to a "FAST" l The Word of God revealed to me, in [Isaiah 58: 61], saying; "is this not the fast that I have chosen; To loose the bonds of wickedness, to undo the heavy burdens, To let the oppressed go free, And that you break every yoke?" Since God called me to this Fast: it was imperative to talk to my doctor concerning "drugs in [5-small pills], that he prescribed for the "protecting of my liver". Because I was taking "SURE CLICK INJECTIONS for a condition call "PASRIASIS!" I felt in my spirit, I should not be taking that medication along with "God's fast!"

As a matter of fact, anyone traveling overseas, you know you much go through custody! However, if you have any medications, you must have an authorized letter, signed by your physician, before you can go thorough custody! The other problem is, the "sure click injections;" must always remain in a cool place! But before the fast began, I thank God, with much Prayer and seeking His face! I needed to talk to the doctor about my medication during this fast! I said Lord what must I do? The "Holy Spirit" moved upon me, to make an appointment to see the doctor. It was two weeks before the fast! After telling my doctor everything; "Thank God the doctor agreed to what "1 wanted to do!" However, he did tell me; "l can't tell you not to take your medications"! But what I am going to do, is have one of my staff workers, call and make an appointment for you to take "Blood Work done, with the date and the time you need to go! He also said, [one week and a half], after the blood work I need you to come to the office!

Readers, we must "thank God for doctors!" Why? Because many people find it difficult to talk about their problems with their doctors. I am so appreciative for the 'Faith in God and, to be self-effacing enough in telling my doctor, exactly how my faith is in 'Christ Jesus!' Because of the truth, he understood my faith! I remembered the leper approaches Jesus and falls upon his face, begging; "Lord, if you just want to, can you make me clean." [Matthew 8:21.

What faith the man has in Jesus Christ! Yes, I have faith also! Because Faith is defined as a complete trust or confidence in someone. Having faith in the love and power of God is doubtful the most major idea of the Bible.

So, after the Fast: I had the blood work done by way of my doctors advise! Therefore, I needed to go to the doctor's office. Of course, I was very weak, and it Was impossible for me to walk alone! I needed someone to help me walk, as well as driving me to the office! I contacted this "wonderful, saved Christian lady, name "Sister Janice." And she drove me to the office in "Riverside, California." I do believe there are many believers in this world have the same faith that I do!

When the doctor came into the room, it was very surprising to me, that he gave me a hug! Then he looked at me saying: "1 have some very, very good news for you!" "Your blood work shows that you do not have to take any of those [five pills per week medication], or those "Sure Clicks injections' anymore! My dear readers, it's impossible to explain how the "Power of God" moved in that office. The only one experience it, besides the doctor Is "The same young lady, Sister, Janice" that drove me to the office! "Whose Report Will You Believe"? "1 shall believe the report of the Lord," [Isaiah 53]! What makes us think that God can't fix what the devil tried to attack: when HE is the one who created our bodies!

DOCTORS TREAT," "GOD HEALS," I am so grateful for all of my "Doctors! Dr. Gary K. Pang, M. D. from Riverside California mentioned that he was privileged enough to know me as his patient. And how he encourages other people to read the book as how "God so melodramatically, and almost matter-factly provided strength and support she needed!"

CHAPTER 2

"PRAYER: AND FAITH WALKING; WORKS!"

If you want to grow in your spiritual walk, you need to make prayer a central part of your life, "with perseverance and petition." The key word here is, Prayer should be made all the time, with all kinds of prayers, for all the saints. So, the possibility of prayer is as wide as the world and as full as the hours in our day. God wants us to bombard the heavenlies with our prayers in a war. An army doesn't fire just one shell or launch one missile at the enemy, they keep firing until it works! Years ago, I wrote "A Prayer Agent Book." For that cause, we do not need to remind God that He is great, gentle, longsuffering, good, kind, and all these things. And we do not need to remind Him that He is all-knowing, all-powerful, even present. God knows what He is, and He knows what we are.

So, how is your prayer life? Is prayer a central and significant part of your life, or is it something you only do when you are with other believers? Is prayer a daily discipline for you, or do you mainly pray when you get in trouble? Do you pray when you are home alone? Or, do you only pray and worship the Lord when you come to church in the presence of others worshiping and praying to God?

To pray regularly requires discipline. Unfortunately, most people are "on-again, off-again" when it comes to prayer. They are faithful for a while, but then they fall out of prayer because they are too tired to come to prayer. They are faithful for a while, but then they fall out of prayer because they are too tired to get up early, or they become distracted by other things.

But how often are we supposed to pray? Ephesians 6:18 gives us the answer! It says, "Praying always with all prayer and supplication in the Spirit and watching thereunto with all perseverance and supplication for all saints." With out Faith it is impossible to please God! [James 2:14-26] says, what good is it, my brothers, if someone says he has faith but does not have works? Can that faith save him? If a brother or sister is poorly clothed and lacking in daily food, and one of you says to them, "Go in peace, be warmed and filled," without giving them the things needed for the body, what good is that?

So also, faith by itself, if it does not have works, is dead. But someone will say, "you have faith and I have works." Show me your faith apart from your works, and I will show you my faith by my works.

This clearly tells us that prayer is not optional for the Christian who is serious about his or her spiritual life. According to this scripture, believers are to make prayer a top priority. Yet, unfortunately, prayer is largely disregarded by the average Christian today! 'Mildred' is suggesting, if prayer isn't priority in your life right now, why not make it a priority starting right now?

You might say, "But I don't have time to pray." You have time to do whatever you really want to do. If it's truly in your heart to pray, you can find the time. And if your schedule is as busy as you think it is, take Ephesians 6:18 to heart. Grab any available time you can find and make it your prayer time. Why not start this day out right?

What about, lets "defeat Satan"! It may not be much fun watching a football game when you already know the final score. But this is exactly the way we need to approach the subject of Satan and his demons. We already know who wins. If we forget that, we may start reacting to Satan as if he were the ultimate winner instead of the ultimate loser. Satan was defeated the instant he rebelled against God. That means he has been a loser for all the ages since that rebellion, and someday he will taste his eternal defeat at the hands of Jesus Christ. As I look at what the Bible says about Satan's defeat, I see ways in which God's Word declares the devil to be a beaten enemy. The first way that Satan was defeated is what I call his strategic defeat. By this 'Mildred' means that he devised a strategy rebellion against God that failed miserably. There was never a second that God's throne was in danger of toppling.

Satan made a poisonous planned mistake in that he, as a creature rebelled against his Creator, the One on whom he depended to sustain his very life. Once upon a time, my son had a dog in the house. Of course, I am afraid of dogs! It would be foolish for the dog to rebel against me, no matter how [scary] I was to him, or how little the dog wants me to be his master. The reason is that I put food in his bowl every day. Every day I pour the dog water to drink. It is because of me that dog could bank on a meal. It is because of me the dog can count on having something to drink. For Satan was even foolish to rebel against God.

Even though the devil is defeated, he can work an optical illusion against us to get us to think he's bigger and more powerful than he really is. Here's what I mean. Let's pretend for a minute that it's OK to look directly at the sun. So, you're looking at the sun, which is so many miles in diameter. But by holding a quarter up close to your eye, then you can block out the sun.

That's what Satan wants us to do, focus on his "quarter"-power; rather than on the awesome power of God. If you focus too much on the devil, he can block you from seeing God. Then you'll get a bigger view of defeating him in the strength God provides.

Instead, God decided to turn Satan's rebellion against him in a way that would bring God more glory. In other words, God is using Satan's rebellion and defeat to display His great glory and accomplish His good plan. In fact, God is using Satan to bring Himself more glory than He would have had if Satan's rebellion had not occurred. You might need to think about All of this for a few minutes. Let Mildred help you with a real-life illustration.

God invited Satan to consider His faithful servant Job. Satan waned to put Job's faith to the test, but he had to get God's permission. We must never forget that, Satan cannot bring anything into your life that God has not reviewed and permitted. Never forget who is in control here. God will permit Satan to test us too. Thank God, "Prayer: And Faith Walking; Works"!

By the way, did you notice the subject of Job's statements? He was focusing on God, not the devil. God is the subject all the way through the book of Job, the issue in Job's trials was not what Satan did, but what God could do. Let's look at the way God used Satan's intentions to bring about His purpose and glory in the life of prideful, independent Peter. God hates pride more than any other sin because it reminds Him of the devil's rebellion.

So, He had to deal with the pride in Peter's heart. Just before Jesus' crucifixion, the Lord stunned Peter by telling him: "Simon, Simon, behold, Satan has demanded permission to sift you like wheat; but I have prayed for you, that your faith may not fail, and you, when once you have turned again, strengthen our brothers (Luke 22:31-32.

Dear readers, if Satan is making your life miserable, the question you need to ask is, "God, why did You give Satan permission to sift me? Remember, that's where "you and I" will find the answer and the way to fix the problem. God gave Satan permission to test peter severely because He knew that when Peter "turned again" and repented, he was going to be a greater minister on God's behalf than he would have been as a prideful, self-confident disciple.

Readers? Does that mean we invite Satan's sifting? I must say, Of course not! But the moment "You and I" say, "That will never happen to me," That's when God gives the devil permission to sift us, because that's pride speaking. I no 'Mildred' is spending extra time on this issue, but it's important. Remember, we're talking about Satan's defeat here, not his Victory. Satan doesn't have any ultimate strategic advantage over us, because he has already been beaten purposefully.

And God not only defeated Satan, He turns Satan's strategy against him. The only thing the devil knows how to do is get us to do what he did, to turn against God in rejection and rebellion. But God will not be out manipulated by the enemy. I can't leave this section without dealing with another classic case of how God uses Satan for His own purposes: Paul's "thorn is the flesh"

(2 Corinthians 12:7). Paul said that this problem, which apparently was some kind of intense physical pain, was "given" to him, yet it was also "a messenger of Satan [sent] to buffer [him]." Paul tells us why: "To keep me from exalting myself! And it includes the 'Author and a lot of you'. Paul struggled with pride. He was a proud man before he got saved, and that pride evidently came over into his Christian experience.

Now he really had something to be proud of, because God had put him at the top of the pile in the church. Paul had received more revelation than any of the other apostles. He was going to write more books of the Bible than any other apostle. He was the only apostle who was transported to heaven and came back to talk about it. He was uniquely blessed, and he had to battle with the pride!

So, God said to Paul, "I am going to help you with your struggle. I am giving Satan permission to bring a problem into your life that is far too big for you to handle." Paul said because the trial was so great, he asked God three times to take it away (2 Corinthians 12:8). But God said, "My grace is sufficient for you, for My power is perfected in your weakness". And Paul made the response.

Before 'Mildred', move to the next method; in which Satan has been defeated, we need to see one other way, in which God uses Satan's rebellion in the lives of His people. It is in the matter of discipline and judgment. A lot of people may not believe God would do that to a person. That's because a lot of people are mixed up on God's relationship to the evil in this world.

God never touches evil Himself, because He is perfectly holy. But God will permit evil forces to do evil. He will give Satan and his demons permission to make someone miserable if that person, like Saul, is living in spiritual rebellion.

Genesis 32:15 also indicates that God's Victory would not come without suffering. The spot of God's righteous Seed on the repair is a puzzling, prophetic way of referring to Jesus' sufferings at His crucifixion. But even though Jesus died, it was Satan who received the deadly blow.

Why? Jesus rose again. A bruise on the heel is not deadly. But Satan got bruised or crushed on the head, which was a death blow. Satan's defeat was announced prophetically in Eden, and it was accomplished at Calvary and with the empty tomb of Jesus Christ. You must understand this view about women, like I did! Because, the strife between the woman's seed and the serpent's seed is unfolded throughout the rest of the Bible. But Let's look at the beginning directly in Genesis 4, how the followers of God and the followers of the devil are engaged in conflict.

Readers, you see when Abel was born, Satan probably thought he was looking at the fulfillment of God's prophecy, the one who would crush his head. Remember, Satan is not all-knowing. He can't see the future, and he can't know God's plan until it is revealed. So, when Satan saw Abel bringing offerings that God accepted, he knew he had to do something to get rid of this seed. So, he put murder in the heart of Cain, and Cain killed his brother Abel (1 John 3:12).

In my studies: let me tell you something about rebelling against God. You can't possible win, not only because God is extremely greater in power, but because He doesn't tell everything. "The secret things belonged to the Lord our God" (Deuteronomy 29:29). God maintained His victorious power.

When Seth was born, Eve herself spoke of the significance of his birth: "God has appointed me another offspring in place of Abel; for Cain killed him." Seth was God's substitute for Abel. Now you see what this has to do with the angelic conflict that began in heaven and was continued on earth. It was in the days of Seth's son Enoch that "men began to call upon the name of the Lord." God had someone else ready to take Abel's place. God always has someone prepared to make sure His will is accomplish.

CHAPTER 3

POWER CAN BREAK FAMILIES STRONGHOLDS

If we are not careful and we give into temptation on a usual basis, a stronghold can form in our "hearts and minds". But if we go against the enemy with God's divine Power we CAN destroy stronghholds. Satan wants you stressing, because When you're not resting in God's ability to care for you. Women tend to stress over things. Whether or not a man will come into your life. And what someone else is saying about us, how our body looks, and so on. Men tend to stress about their jobs, providing for their families, and whether or not they are "making the cut" in several areas of life. It's amazing how many people profess to know God and follow Him, Yet their thinking patters are just like those of anyone else in the world. Satan loves that. He wants you to be so fascinated with the ways of the world that you are new about what Gods word said. Be a student of God's Word. What does the Bible say about this problem that I am facing? Be prepared to face the Devil., Those strongholds are how the Devil wants to keep us as his prisoners!

Sometimes this requires that children be reminded who is in charge. Kids need to understand that obedience is crucial to their well-being as well as the wellbeing of the home. Don't let Satan use our children to build a stronghold. "the author is saying [Fight for your family]! Genesis 3:15 says that Jesus Christ would give Satan a blow to his head, and Satan would never be the same again. That blow was delivered on the cross of Calvary, so keep on fighting for your family. Satan does not have any right to build his strongholds in your family if you are under the blood of Jesus Christ. Let me tell you that If you will use the weapons of God on Satan, he won't know what hit him!

Satan has lost the fight, but he's still taking prisoners and hauling in the drape. Don't let him add your family to his account. Don't let him take you and your family as spoils when he's the loser and you're the winner in Jesus Christ. I want to close this chapter with a word of encouragement for you. After Adam and Eve let Satan wreck their lives through sin, God did a gracious thing. He drove the man and woman He created out of Eden and put angels at the entrance to guard it lest they return. God acted kindly by driving Adam and Eve out. Why?

Because God didn't want them to eat of the tree of Life and live forever in their sinful state with no hope of redemption. He ejected them for Eden, but they left with the promise of a coming redeemer ringing in their ears. That Redeemer came and died on another tree, the cross of Calvary.

That's good news for you and your family. That means no matter how deeply Satan has penetrated your home, no matter the devastation he has wrought on your marriage and in the lives of your children, because of that other tree, the Cross, you have hope in God's salvation. Although Adam and Eve didn't get to taste the fruit of the Tree of Life because of sin, we who know Jesus Christ have enjoyed the fruit of the tree called the Cross. If you will establish this other tree, the cross of Christ, in our home, there will be no room left for Satan's strongholds. ":Power And Faith Can Break Strongholds!"

The Bible is clear that Satan can build his strongholds in the lives of individuals and families. The devil knows if he can weaken the church internally, he can weaken in witness. So, let 'Mildred' give some examples of what I mean. The Church is under the stronghold of discord. Many individual churches are being held by strongholds such as ongoing conflict and bitterness: that in some cases have affected several generations of their members. We can have examples of church strongholds in the New Testament. The church at Corinth. Revelation [2:18-29]. An evil woman the risen Christ called Jezebel.

Before we talk, it was revealed to me that this is why some Christian wives need to "repent of their rebellious attitudes", toward their "husband's authority." If a wife wants God to change her husband, she needs to" honor his position." My prayer and thanks to God for wifes" that shows respect to her husband in any, "positions that God has given to him!" If you give respect, then you will receive respect! Why is this a big deal with God? First, because it reflects the order He established. And second, because we are talking about spiritual warfare and satanic strongholds. Satan is so strong that even the "Archangel Michael" didn't rebuke him. We need the weapons of God to defeat the devil.

The Bible also addresses husbands. "Husbands, love your

wives and do not be unpleasant against them" [Colossians 3:19]. Some men have attitude problems too. Some men think wives are spirits that appear magically out of a lamp, bow, and say, "your wish is my command." Wives are partners, not servants, How can you know husband, if you are loving your wife? It's simple. What are you sacrificing for her? Loving your wife like Christ loved the church [Ephesians 5:25] involves sacrifice. Since Mildred was married to a wonderful man too! let me put it this way gentlemen! Make sure that at the end of the day, you have made more deposits than withdrawals in your "wife's emotional and spiritual account." Men have the tendency to come home and want to know what's for dinner and why it isn't ready yet. We want our wives to do this and that and meet our needs, and we are regularly making withdrawals from their accounts. Then we wonder why the account is empty.

Wives need emotional and spiritual nourishment. They need love, attention, help with the kids. They need you to listen to them and care about the things that are affecting them. It would transform a lot of Christian marriages if the husband would simply ask himself this question; "What deposits can I make in my wife's account today?" If he will make an effort to make those deposits, a husband will find that they accrue interest. And Satan will have one less door of access into the home.

Since we know that "Your Faith Can Break Families Strongholds," It's probably safe to say that you know at least, one family that ready has fallen apart, is falling apart or is functioning far below what God intended the family to be. The family you know may even be yours. Some families suffer because the relationship between the husband and wife has become paralyzed. Other families are hurting because rebellious children are causing grief. Still, other families are suffering because some members are reaping a harvest of trouble from the sins committed by an earlier generation. All of these problems and more can easily become strongholds that Satan builds to get a grip on the family and keep it from being everything God intended the family to be. The tragedy is that many families batting satanic strongholds decide that the fight is no longer worth the grief, so they want to throw in the towel and give up. Spouses head for divorce court because they don't see any solution to their dilemma. Satan is definitely in a "building boom" today in erecting family strongholds. He knows what he is doing because he has been at it for a long time. He built his first stronghold in the first family in history. And he did it right in the middle of the Garden of Eden, God's paradise. Let's look at the method Satan used to drive a wedge into the family of Adam and Eve. The fall of Adam and Eve and the subsequent problems in their family were caused by an attack from the fallen spirit world. Satan infiltrated the first home and disrupted it. His attack caused spiritual deterioration in the lives of Adam and Eve, which led to a relational deterioration in their family.

We know that this sin resulted in a family stronghold because it carried over to the next generation when Can killed Abel' This wasn't just a one-time thing Satan's infiltration of Adam's family became the foundation for murder. So we can raise the first family breakup and the first family stronghold to the work of the fallen angel world. And we could say that every family breakup can be traced to the the same fallen angel world. And we could say that every family breakup can be traced to the same source. Because Satan's premier goal, next to destroying you, is the destruction of your family. What was the methodology Satan used to infiltrate the family of Adam and Eve and build his stronghold? Satan's method was simple. He got Adam and Eve to reverse their biblical roles and responsibilities. We could summarize what Satan told Eve in the first five verses of Genesis 3 with two statements; "You don't need God. And you don't need Adam." Satan got Eve to act independently of God. He tempted her to use her own reasoning and her own logic to reverse God's order and to think in terms of independence. Satan then Influenced Adam to become a passive male and stand on the sidelings.

Eve took over the leadership. Adam became the submissive responder, the roles were reversed, and Satan had an open door.

Whenever roles are reversed in marriage, a context whereby Satan can infiltrate the home. Marriage conflict was the result of the role reversal in the first family. The failure of Eve to remain in her role, and the failure of Adam to take his rightful role of leadership, opened the door for the devil to take over both roles, and it was a disaster for the family, According to Genesis 3:7, Adam and Eve had to sew fig leaves together to cover themselves, for they became ashamed of each other and of themselves. Now, instead of openness and authenticity, there was hiddenness and secrets. In the encounter with God and the judgment that followed, both parties passed the blame to someone else. Adam, who had been so excited about Eve just a few verses earlier, now said to God, "It's her fault." And Eve fingered the serpent. The curse God pronounce in Genesis 3:14-19 was staggering. Notice that there would be conflict in the home, God said to eve, "Your husband... shall rule over you" [v.16]. In other words, men would seek to control women by domination. As evil as it is, as wrong as it is, men would seek to dominate women and not lead lovingly. And the desire of the woman for relationship and for partnership would become a battle rather than a blessing.

God cursed the ground for the man so that from then on, he would come home tired from a day of trying to wrestle a living out of a stubborn earth. Instead of coming home to serve his wife, he would come home expecting to be served by her, and that would produce conflict. And after all this, Adam and Eve had to endure the murder of one son by another son. Satan's infiltration of the families for generations. He will use any means he can to maggot his way into a family and create havoc. How does Satan work his way into a family and build strongholds? I'm not just talking about a family having an occasional argument or some other conflict. I'm talking about a situation in which a family is imprisoned by a problem it can't break free of. Satan uses a number of means to bring about family breakdown and the building of strongholds. Let's discuss a few of the most important and most common so we can learn how to tear down what Satan has constructed.

There are a lot of angry people out there-angry at parents, mates, children, or even themselves, for things that have happened, If a wrong has been committed against you, you have a right to be angry. The Bible says that the Lord is angry with the wicked every day [Psalm 7:11] KJV, Anger at sin is valid. But prolong anger violates the scriptural command to resolve it quickly and it provides the ground Satan needs to build that unresolved anger into a stronghold. Paul says it clearly in [Ephesians 4:27]. Lingering anger becomes an opportunity for Satan. It gives the enemy the unlocked door he needs to break into your home and do his destructive work. Ask the Holy Spirit for guardians. That's one way to tear down an anger stronghold in your family. Another way is to seek forgiveness from others if you are the offender. Then when Satan tries to get you to play that old anger videotape, serve notice on him that in the name of Jesus Christ, that tape has been ejected. Of course, Satan will come back more than once trying to play that tape on the VCR of your heart and mind. But all you have to do is push the eject button each time by claiming your position in Christ and reminding the devil that the anger has been forgiven and laid to rest.

Rebellion is another powerful weapon Satan uses to disturb families and build strongholds. Rebellion simply means to go against God's established order of authority. Satan was the original rebel, so it's not surprising that he would attempt to form rebellion in the family. Rebellious children can tear a family apart as quickly as anything. So can adults who refuse to submit themselves to God's legitimate chain of command. In fact I want to spend most of my time here dealing with the adults, because God said in [Exodus 20:51 that if we would pass the results of disobedience on to the 'third and fourth' generation. Parents can hand their children and grandchildren over to a real untidiness when they rebel against God's authority. Some Christians are setting in motion a pattern of rebellion that will have generational consequences if the pattern is not reversed.

Before we talk about specific examples of rebellion, I

want us to see how seriously God takes the sin of rebellion. The Apostle Peter has some strong words about rebellion as it relates to the angelic conflict and then to people who have joined in that rebellion against God. Peter writes, "God did not spare angels when they sinned. [2 Peter 2:41. The line of these angels was that they joined Satan in his rebellion. The people of Noah's day and the citizens of Sodom and Gomorrah can also be classified as rebels. Peter reminds us that God also brought judgment Against the world of Noah's day, and against Gomorrah. Then Peter says, "The Lord knows how to keep the righteous under punishment for the day of judgment." But then in verses 10-12, Peter apply the principle of God's judgment to the false teaches of his day. Notice a few traits of these people. They "indulge the flesh in its corrupt desires, despise authority, and self-willed." They are also not afraid to "revile angelic majesties." Any place where we yield ground, Satan becomes a potential location for one of his strongholds.

If Satan can deceive us into thinking that we worship an important, powerless Savior who can do nothing for us, then he can keep a church Spiritually bloodless. That's why it is the task of the pastor and the leadership of the church to proclaim Christ with authority. Not to preach "sermonettes" for Christianity, Messages like that have authority and little passion. But if we serve a "little God," what do we really have to say? I once got an invitation to speak at a church and was told that the pastor normally preached "A ten-minute sermon."

I'm not comparing a church's spirituality with the

length of the pastor's sermons. All the "Author" can say, "That's not me!" "What I am sayig," if we're not careful, we can reduce God to our size and "fit Him into our convenience." When that happens, the church is held 'hostage' to a secular way of thinking. How do we tear down strongholds in the church? The place to begin, is with the "Lord and Head of the church with His message to the people" who make up His body. In the opening chapters of the book of Revelation, we meet the risen Jesus Christ in all of His power and glory. When was the last time the church had such an overwhelming vision of Jesus that we fell at his feet like dead people? If we can come into the presence of God and the church, we'll never be overcomer, then we don't know who we're dealing with. The Lord whom John saw had a message concerning the future, and that is the majority of the Revelation. But Jesus also had a message for the present, to His church.

He told John, "Write in a book what you see and send it to the seven churches" [Revelationl:ll]. In "Biblical numerology," the number seven is "perfection or completion." It was also His complete message to all churches in this age.

After all of my researching, This message was released in the "Authors heart" to "write about this in the book !

"What are you teaching your children at home?" As parents, we have a responsibility to train and prepare our children to be successful in life! And there is no better classroom for teaching them the responsibilities of that life in our homes. God expects us to teach our children how to conduct themselves, how to respond to authority, how to cooperate with others, how to work as a part of a team, and how to successfully execute daily responsibilities. By giving our children this kind of training, we prepare them for the real world where they will one day be employed and make a living. This issue of properly training our children is extremely important! In first Timothy 3:4, the Apostle Paul wrote that leaders are to set the example in this area for everyone else in the church. A leader must be "one that ruleth well in his own house, having his children in subjection with all seriousness."

I was the "Youth director" for 'all ages', in the "Youth department," at my home church in "Compton California." As a matter of fact, I had hands on—with Many youngest, as well as my own children! Therefore, I want to focus on what Paul said that applies to all children, for there are no double standards. We are commanded by God to train, teach, prepare, and equip our sons and daughters victoriously; into the arena of their lives! Paul also said, that our children should be "train subjection with all importances." The word "subjection," means to set things in order or to be subject to someone else, and it strongly suggests the idea of obedience to authority.

It is important that Paul uses this word when speaking to parents, for it affirms that parents have the right to exercise godly authority over their children, If children don't voluntarily submit! Remember, parents have every right before God to force their children to obey. Further confirming the strength of a military term that was used to describe soldiers who were under the command or authority of a superior officer. Let's consider how this example of a soldier in the military applies to the training of our own children.

I have a family member that was in the military! Plus I learned a lot about military, when I "ran a meeting in Germany on the base." "A soldier knows from the first day who is in charge and to whom he reports. Having this knowledge clears away any confusion about who he is accountable to. He has been given clear instructions about who is the boss, and this sets things in order so he never has to wonder who is really in charge.

Likewise parents need to make it clear from the time a child is young that "Dad and Mom" are the boss! And they are the ultimate authority in the home! When a parent doesn't exercise authority and lets child get away with whatever he or she wants, it brings confusion into the home. Set things straight by making it known to your children that you are the one that demands godly role as the leader of your house. By teaching children to respond correctly to your authority at home, you are preparing them to respond properly to their future employers as well.

For example, the soldier understands that he is expected to fulfill these basic duties each day---duties such as making his/her bed, combing your hair, grooming our face, shining his shoes, and wearing clothes that are pressed.

Likewise, your children need daily duties to teach them responsibilities. Paul is telling us that, like soldiers, children need daily discipline including responsibilities that are required an expected of, each day. This kind of "basic training" helps children to understand the realities of work, life, and how to be a part of a team, In the real world, no one will do everything for them when they are an adult. They will get a big shock when they go out into the world and suddenly discovers that no one is going to be "easy on them in the workplace," and they has to carry their weight of responsibility. That's why, "Gods Power can Break Families Strongholds!

CHAPTER 4

"SPEAK TO YOURSELF IN THE LAST DAYS"

Many years ago, when I was speaking at a church, the pastor informed me that the Church seems to be going backwards, instead of going forward in the Lord! This really amazed me to hear information's like that! Friends, your "Author" was not defeated, "because off what I have experience at that time." The Holy Spirit was letting me know that these are "The last days!" Therefore, when we are going in and out different placers, doing "Field Work," We must always be "Prayed up, listening to the voice of God" The Bible makes it clearly plain that in the last days, the world will be filled with difficulties, of which we have never been before known in the history of mankind. In fact, the [The Holy Spirit] was committed to making sure we understand what will occur in the last days [Second Timothy 3:1], it is as if He points His prophetic finger two thousand years into the future and exactly foretells what will occur at the end of the age. Paul wrote these words by inspiration of the Holy Spirit in [2nd Timothy 3:11] "This know also that in the last days perilous times shall come."

In the city of "Thessalonica" were undergoing horrifying persecution. The precautioning in this city was worse than it was in other places because Christians were being disturbed both by pagan idol worshipers and by unbelieving Jews who detested the Gospel Message. Because of these threatening conditions, members of the Thessalonian church were suffering, and some even paid the price of dying for the Gospel. However, in place of these afflictions and pressures from outside forces, this congregation refused to surrender to defeat us to figure out our deliverance by ourselves! He took it one step further and gave us the secret weapon for jerking those roots clear out of the ground and sending them to a place where they will never again produce their wicked fruit in us. Jesus said, "If ye had faith as a grain of mustard seed, ye might say unto this cycamore tree, be thou plucked up by the root, and be thou planted in the sea; and it should obey you" [Luke 17:61.] Jesus specifically said that you must literally speak to the sycamore tree, In other words, this isn't a person who mumbles thoughtless nonsense; this is a person who has made an inward resolution and now speaks convincingly and with great conviction. Your voice represents your authority; therefore, when you raise your voice, you release your authority.

That is why you must speak to these attitudes and not just think about them. You can think them. But when you get so tired of live-in under the stress and strain of bitterness, unforgiveness, and offers that you lift your voice and command these foul forces to go, they will finally begin to obey you! Those poisonous root in your life, but your thoughts will not remove them. I promise you, friend, if you wait until you feel like speaking to those ugly attitudes, you'll never do it. If you depend on your feelings and emotions to motivate you, you'll never be free of offense and unforgiveness. Your feelings and emotions will tell you that you have a right and a reason to feel the way you do. Your flesh will talk you into hanging on to those unprofitable, harmful attitudes. So, make the choice not to listen to your negative emotions anymore; then start exercising your Godgiven authority by speaking to yourself in this Last Day!

It is time for you to accept personal responsibility for your inward condition. Stop blaming everyone else for all your bad attitudes and acknowledge that there is something inside you that needs to be removed! Jesus said you must speak to that "sycamore tree" and tell it to go!

- If you don't speak to your emotions, they will speak to you.
- If you don't take authority, they will take authority over you.
- If you don't rise and conquer our flesh, it will conquer you!
- So, quit letting your emotions tell you what to think, do, and how to react.
- It's time for you to do the talking, take command of your own thought life!

If the Holy Spirit speaks to you and tells you to do something specific, then obey Him! Do you remember when the death angel passed through Egypt and took the firstborn of all the Egyptians? The reason Israel was unaffected was that the Israelites obeyed the instructions God gave them to put blood on the doorposts of their houses. They brushed that lamb's blood on the doors of their houses just as God had ordered. Later when the death angel came, he passed by every home where there was blood on the doorposts. In the end, not one of the Israelites was touched! As we obey the Word of God and listen to the Holy Spirit's leading, we will have wisdom to know every step we need to take in the days ahead. All we must do is obey God's instructions, and He guarantees us blessing and provision even in difficult times. But if we try to take another approach, there is no guarantee for us to claim. We must do what God says if we want to be assured of His divine blessing and protection.

As a spiritual leader and friend, 'Mildred' want to encourage you to increase your level of faith, especially if you are facing challenging times. Stand on the Word of God; exercise your faith; listen to the Holy Spirit; and obey what He tells you to do. As you do these things, God's supernatural blessings will kick into action, and you will soon find a river of supernatural provision flowing to you. It would be helpful to close this chapter with a personal inventory.

Which of these four works are you because you have not yet trusted Christ? Then trust Him now! Have you experienced His work for you [in you and through you]? Are you wearing the "graveclothes" or the "grace-clothes?" Are you enjoying the liberty you have in Christ, or are you still bound by the habits of the old life in the graveyard of sin? As a Christian, you have been raised and seated on the throne. Practice your position in Christ! He has worked for you; now let Him work in you and through you, that He might give you an exciting, creative life to the glory of God.

CHAPTER 5

"SUPERNATURAL REVELATION SOLVES PROBLEM"

Many years ago, I was preaching in a series of meetings about the power of the Holy Spirit. At the end of one of the services, an invitation was given for people to come forward who wanted to be filled with the Spirit, I watched with great joy how people filled the altar of that church. They slipped down on their knees, lowered their heads in prayer, and began to ask the Lord to touch them, to fill them, and in some cases, to refill them with a fresh infilling of power.

As we stepped down to pray for the people, one off the head 'Prayer warriors' said to me, "Evangelist, you can rest." I will be praying for them to night. I moved aside, with much respect. You see, when you are in someone else's Pulpit. Although the Power of the "Holy Spirit" is still moving and speaking, with that "supernatural Revelation solves Problems!" So, then I let him take the lead, but it was a bad decision he made! Because, I watched as this leader moved among those dear people, patting them on the back and telling them, "You have to pray louder: You have to pray harder: You have to plead if you want to be filled. You have to tarry a little longer." Later, after service,

I asked the head prayer warrior, how long have these people been praying to be filled with the Spirit? He said that some had been waiting for years! I was shocked! I thought to myself, why has it taken so long for these believers to be filled with the Holy Spirit when this is something God has made available to every believer? God wants us to receive it. He knows we need it to walk-in victory, to exercise authority in our lives, and to overcome the works of the devil.

But where do we get that supernatural power? Paul answers this question in Ephesians 5:10, "Finally, my brethren, be strong in the Lord, and in the power of his might." Readers, you can't get this supernatural power by reading books or listening to tapes, the books and tapes can direct you to the place where it can be found, but the power itself can only be gotten through a personal relationship with the Lord Jesus Christ. This power is locked up "in the Lord." now, let me take this one step further so I can explain why it's so easy and uncomplicated for you to receive a new infilling of God's power in your life.

Paul is saying we have been placed inside Jesus Christ; He has become our kingdom of life and the place of our residence. Let 'Mildred" give an example, just like you are living at a certain physical address, you also have a spiritual address. You permanently reside-inside the 'Son of God'! He is your permanent home. A home from which you will never move because you are locked up in a securely place inside Him continually! Please, stay with me, because this now leads us to the reason that the "supernatural Revelation solves problems!"

I remember one January day several years ago when I awakened from my sleep very early in the morning, and I sensed that the Holy Spirit was awaking me because there was something He wanted to tell me. At first, I thought I was just having a difficult time sleeping, so I tried to wave it off and go back to sleep. But the longer I laid there in my bed, the more I became aware that it was God who was stirring up my spirit. There was something He wanted to say to me. For months preceding that time, I had been seeking answers to some very important questions about the steps I needed to take to fulfill the assignment God had given to me. I had spent hours thinking over these questions I faced.

I had worked my ink pen over endless pages that were jotted with my notes. Yet I couldn't find the right answer to the questions that remained constantly on my mind. I had prayed and prayed about it, but it seemed that the correct answers kept dodging me. Then in the early hours of the morning, the answers suddenly came! I walked back and forth in my room, as I prayed. Finally, I went to my table where I always do my writing, laid my head on it, and pray more earnestly!

I said "Holy Spirit, what is it that You want to reveal to me this morning? What is it that You want to communicate to me?" Suddenly, and very unexpectedly, it seemed as if the spiritual realm miraculously opened, and a stream of information descended from Heaven and began to pour the answers needed directly into my mind! As that information began rolling into my mind, I instantly saw the solutions for which I had been seeking for so long! Friends of mine, this was not the first time I'd had that experience. The Holy Spirit had revealed many times to me through the years, and I know, He will continue to be my unlimited Source, that, "Supernatural Revelation Solves problems"!

Consider our own lives. Are you experiencing victory in most areas of your life, or are you suffering defeat in key areas? Have you ignored the fact that spiritual Warfare is real? Have you gathered outs of spiritual information, knowledge, and facts, yet forgotten to put on the whole armor of God?

Well, praise God for all the knowledge you've gained, but now it's time to turn your intelligent knowledge of God's Word into the sword of the Spirit. Then you must raise it high and wave it against the attacks the enemy has been trying to bring against you, It's also time for you to turn your knowledge about faith into a protection that withstands every demonic attack!

So, "Don't Disqualify Yourself!" Scripture said: "But I keep under my body and bring it into subjection: lest that by any means, when I have preached to others, I myself should be a castaway [1 Corinthians 9:27]. Readers, we need to take notice to the Word of God, because recent years, have been painful for the worldwide Christian community as they have witnessed famous Christian leaders fall into sin time and again. A long time ago, I was out of town, conducting services in "another state, not to mention where! My adjutant an I, sat in my hotel room and watched with a broken heart as a famous evangelist, whose voice once touched the nations! Because sin in his personal life had become public information years earlier, his words now seem empty, hollow, and irrelevant,

To me, one of the saddest things in the world is to see a man or woman whom God once powerfully used to preach the Gospel to the people, fall into sin! People often make the tragic mistake of thinking that just because they have been Successful in the past, they will continue to be successful in the future. But I have known many ministers of the gospel who once experienced great success in the ministry and then slowly allowed their fire to go out. Whether they fell into sin or just became tired and complacent, the result was the same: They lost the cutting edge they once possessed in their ministries. The primary reason people become discredited and shamed is that they don't control their flesh. Instead of crucifying the flesh and submitting it to the control of the Holy Spirit, they pander to the cravings of the flesh. As a result, they become dominated by the desires of the flesh, and those fleshly desires very misleadingly lead them to fall into sin.

Paul was a great apostle who was filled with divine revelation and had preached to more people than anyone else in this day. Nevertheless, one off the greatest concerns was that after doing all he had done for the kingdom, he might later become a "castaway!" Paul didn't consider himself so high and mighty that he couldn't imagine this happening to him. Rather than make the mistake others had made by letting his flesh get the best of him, ultimately destroying both him and his status, Paul acted with great determination to keep his flesh under control. He must remember that "Supernatural Revelation Solves Problems!"

Readers, if you continue going the way you are going right now, in your physical body, it is going to be a perfected tool that God can use, or is it going to lead your flesh into problems? Make sure you don't become a castaway after all the good you have already done! Keep believing that, "Supernatural Revelation Solve Problems!" other people are often difficult and empty about the most important things, while pouring energy and love into solving what is often unsolvable." God is saying "I am with you;" because "Supernatural Revelation Salving Problems!" I remember, God said tell my people, "I'm with you for a purpose!" In other words, your important sufferings don't happen by accident." But we often misuse God's sovereignty when it comes to helping sufferers, both ourselves and others!

[I, the author of this book], is a woman of "articulate Faith!" I am honest about the pain of loss! But my God speaks the final key word about me; that is, "I will carry you and never let you go." That is perhaps the deepest comfort communicated by "God's spoken Word."

I hear the Lord saying, I will never fail you, Keep the faith! 'Our gracious Lord' uses the outward sufferings as a substance to free you from the enemy within. Like aged can bring us into the shadow of death, and finally you will be accepted into the darkness of the last enemy, why is this? Because like so many in the Church world today, the Ephesian believers had gathered together a huge gathering of spiritual knowledge, information, and facts; never less, this alone was not enough to keep the devil under their feet where he belonged! As we read through Ephesian we can see that the devil was apparently attacking the Ephesian church and was having some success! But remember; "Supernatural Revelation Solves problems!

That's why Paul had to instruct these believers to put away lying, steal no more, let no corrupt communication out of their mouths, grieve not the Holy Spirit, and put aside all anger and malice. Does this sound like a church full of victorious people to you? They are overcoming, abundant life that Jesus Christ had come to offer them. The reason God's power is so addressable to us is that both we and this divine power are gloriously locked up inside the same place!

Let "Mildred" use a simple illustration to help you get the point of what I'm communicating to you now. For a long time, I had a huge 'aquarium' in my bed room!" It was a pleasure to see; the water bubbling and the fishes, swimming from top to bottom, as well as: from side to side! It gave me "Supernatural Revelation about my own life!" The fact that we exist in inside, 'Jesus along with God's power' can be somewhat likened to "water and fish" sharing the same space in an aquarium. The water and fish are different in substance", but they both reside in the same tank. The tank serves as the "home" for these two substances that are held alongside within its walls. Therefore, the fish doesn't have to release its faith to get into the water, for it already continually lives in the water.

The very fact that we are locked up inside the Lord along with the Holy Spirit's supernatural power, means that we are never far away form a new surge of superhuman power into our human spirits. A fresh surge of this power into us is as accessible as our very next breath of air! It's just as normal for us to receive a new infilling of the Spirit as it is for a fish to freely swim around in its tank.

In fact, God has designed our lives in Christ in such a way

that it would be very difficult for us not to freely receive this impartation of superhuman,

"Supernatural Strength" for the fight. However, if we're to experience this ever available, ever near power, we must open our hearts to it and ask God to release it into our lives. Then by faith we must reach out to embrace it.

This means there is no need to beg, plead, or beat yourself up in prayer to somehow prove that you are good enough to receive this divide power. If you know Jesus Christ, you are already locked up in the same place with the power of God. In fact, you're rubbing elbows with it all the time. It's no more difficult to receive than it is for a "fish to start swimming"! It's ours for the taking! So, let us Thank God for his "Supernatural Revelation Solves Problems!"

CHAPTER 6

"JESUS'S MESSAGE TO THE CHURCH"

I remembered when my "Pastor" "Dr. Reuben P. Anderson," assigned the "Youth Department" over to me. As well as helping the "Missionary Department." At that time, I was attending the "California Baptist Collage." It was very important to me, that these Departments, would understand all the guidelines about their responsibilities in each department, teaching in different sections! Then it was important for me to outline some ideas, that will better help them to understand, "What the "Message of Jesus Christ" is all about to the Church!

"Lets look at the "Message About Love." So what does Jesus say to the church? Read [Revelation 2:24], I know your deeds and your toil and perseverance, and that you cannot endure evil Men and you, put to test those who call themselves apostles, and they are not, and you have found them to be false, and you have perseverance and have endured for My name's sake, and have not grown weary. But I have this against you, that you have left your first love.

It is necessary to have correct doctrine. But correct doctrine ought to help us to love Christ more. It's right to take a stand for the truth. But the truth should make us more passionate to know Christ intimately. If you know more now then you did last year, and yet you are enjoying your spiritual life less, your priorities are off. The Bible compares our relationship with Christ to a marriage: The partners in a marriage can be faithful to each other, yet can have a passionless marriage. One reason for this is that most people date in order to marry when they ought to be marrying in order to date! Let me tell you why that is? Because, after marriage people you should continue caring about each other, spending time together, and paying attention to each other. A man should want to study his mate.

People who quit dating after they marry often get bored. "Mildred" can tell you much more! They wonder what happened to the fire. The fire went out because the relationship is backward. When you marry in order to date, you have a driver designed to keep the passion of the relationship alive. That's how it should be in the church's with Christ. Satan can gain ground in the church when we leave our first love for Jesus Christ. "Love is the "Message for the Church,"

Now, Lets talk about "A message about faithfulness". In [Revelation 2:9-10], this is the word! I know our tribulation and your poverty [but you are rich], and the blasphemy by those who say they agree jews are not, but are a synagogue of Satan. Do not fear what you are about to suffer. Behold, the devil is about to cast some of you into prison, that you may be tested, and you will have tribulation ten days. "Be faithful to Me no matter what. Don't quit standing up for Me when the going gets tough. Don't be convenience-loving church made up of convenience-loving Christians who only serve Me when they are being blessed."

The believers in Smyrna were going through hard times. Many of them were poor, and they were facing persecution by a group of people energized by Satan. It would have been easy for the church in smyrna to throw in the towel and let Satan have the victory he sought. A lot of people are willing to follow Jesus as long as they are getting Christmas blessings. Everybody likes a God who gives out goodies, who simply invites people to "name it and claim it." But Jesus has called us to take up our cross and follow Him [Mark 8:34].

A cross is an instrument to suffering. We can't follow Jesus only during the good times and call ourselves the church. We must be faithful to Him even when following Him involves suffering. When times are good, they are good because God is good. But even when times are bad, God is still good. The Church's job is to obey Christ faithfully, not to please everybody. Some churches get criticized a lot because they practice things like church discipline. People will say, "What right do you have getting into other people's business? Well, it would be a lot easier not to practice church discipline. It would save us a lot of headaches. The only problem is, the Lord has not given us that option. He commands the church to apply discipline where it is needed, and we have to obey.

In my studies, It talks about the church is not on earth to win friends and influence people. It's just a choice between standing for Christ and winning popularity! When that discussion came up, I believe in my heart, there's only one choice the church can make. We are called to be faithful no matter what, and when we do that Jesus will take care of the rest! "Because, "Theses are Jesus's Messages to the Church!" Readers, even now in [20181, we live in a 'day of quitters'! People bail out of their marriages when times get tough. People leave the church when things don't go the way they like! Many people today are ready to quit the minute the heat is on. But Jesus says, "If you want to know My power and spiritual authority, stand firm in trouble and I will make you an overcomer." That's the message of "faithfulness"

Let's look at "A message about Compromise." The church must address compromise when it happens because God has called us to a higher standard. The church is to be visibly different. Believers are to be joined in marriage or other close partnerships with unbelievers because, as Paul asks, "What fellowship has light with darkness?" The answer is, none. {2 corinthians 6:14]. The Bible calls it being "joined with an unbeliever cooperation". I know it sound radical today, but the biblical standard often seems radical when it is held up to the, "anything goes" standards of our culture.

Parents, Mildred has a question for you!. What do you tell your children when they tell you everybody else is doing something? You tell them, "Well, you're not everybody else, And in this house, we don't do that." That's what Joshua meant when he declared, "As for me and my house, we will serve the Lord" [Joshua 24:15). The church needs to confess compromise as a sin. The Lord was pictured speaking to this church with a sharp, two-edged sword coming out of His mouth. The sword is His Word, the only thing that can cut out the cancer of compromise. We have to start saying, "Compromise is sin. And by God's grace, we are going to cut it out of the body and soul!."

Lets look at a "Message about Holiness." The people at Thyatira had some good things going for them. They had grown in their faith and love and service to the Lord. But the church had a major problem in its midst, a woman the Lord called Jezebel. "All of us heard about her"! However, that may not have been this woman's actual name, but in using the name Jezebel, Jesus picture her on the image of Israel's wicked, devious, bossy queen who manipulated her husband, King Ahab, and everyone else. Jezebel ran the show. She was out of her placed because she was ruling the church, something God does not allow a woman to do [1Timothy 2:11-121. She was teaching false doctrine. This woman with rebellion, gave herself the title "prophetess," But that only masked her sin.

Please, let me mention something here. I realize that a church, with a lot of outreaches and ministries, cannot promise for the religious soundness and personal holiness of every person who walks through those doors. But that's entirely different from allowing mess-up people to go public in the church with their messed-up doctrine and lifestyles. Jezebel had gone public with her heresy and wickedness because she was teaching it to everybody else. And what's worse, the church was tolerating her. No one was dealing with the problem:. "l pray we would take notice to these statements!" No one was speaking out against her rebellion and sin. It's pretty easy for Satan to build a stronghold in the church when the church invites his children inside and gives them a hammer and nails.

The church cannot tolerate unholiness, because God will not tolerate it. The Bible said, I know your deeds, that you have a name that you are alive, but you are dead. Wake up, and strengthen the things that remain, which were about to die; for I have not found your deeds completed in the sight of My God. Remember therefore what you have received and heard; and keep it, and repent' If therefore you will not wakeup, I will come like a thief, and will not know at what hour I will come upon you [Revelation 3:1-3].

Jesus was addressing a sleeping church. It's hard to move forward when you're asleep, Why do some churches fail to make progress? One reason is that they are living off what God did yesterday. Watch out for a church where all the people can talk about what God did in the good old days, how things use to be around there. The church at Sardis didn't have much left, and even the things that remained were about to go up. This church was stuck. The problem with this, is that you can't stand still in the spiritual life. You are impartial.

Do you have trouble waking up in the morning? Many people do. Sometimes I do! How may have to drag yourself out of bed in the morning and totter around trying to regain awareness. But even if you have a hard time waking up, you still get up every morning. Why? Even though you don't like getting up, you know that if you don't, you will soon lose your job and starve. The fact that you showed up at work last week won't put food on your table this week.

The wonderful things the church did for God yesterday are history. They are in the past. Of course, we should celebrate them and thank God for them and build on them, but we can't relive them.; We can't recapture the past. The same goes for the mistakes the church made yesterday. We need to learn from past mistakes so we don't repeat them, but we also can't linger over them. That's why Paul said he forgot the things that were behind him and pressed forward to the things ahead of him. He was after the prize of God's "Well done," and he didn't want the past weighing him down !

You see, living in the past is like trying to drive while staring in the rearview mirror of your car. You move forward by focusing on the windshield, not the rearview mirror. "I praise God for giving me revelations of things!" All of my readers know this;" Notice how large your windshield is compared to your rearview mirror. The windshield covers a lot more territory because the object of driving is to move forward. You only need to glance back every one in a while to avoid making a mistake while you're moving forward. Satan wants to keep the church focused on the rear-view mirror of yesterday so we won't pay attention to where we're going today. Jesus says, "Wake up, open your eyes, and move on to tomorrow."

Now, lets look at the, "message about Obedience".We don't need to blow this point. We have seen again the importance of obedience to God in pursuing successful spiritual warfare. This church kept God's Word even though Satan was harassing the believers through the people in one of his "synagogues." Satan was trying to build a stronghold in the church, but the people wouldn't allow it if you want to tear down strongholds in any of these categories on earth, you must be able to address the problem from the standpoint of heaven. Let me define the four terms Paul uses in [Colossians 1] because they are general in countryside

They have to do with the community the world around us. We all no that, "A throne is a chair of authority." Kings and queens sit on thrones. America doesn't have a throne, but we have a chair of authority. It's the "Executive chair the president" occupies in the "Oval Office of the White house." America's territory includes the fifty states and the grounds our nation rules around the world. Because of "MY" husbands position in "government and it's territories," I have a good understandings of many things that "I dear not mention!"

However, Here is another term Paul used in [Colossians is rulers. A ruler is a specific person who occupies a place of authority, whether that person be the mayor, the government the president, the chairman of the board, the king or queen, or whatever. Rulers sit on throne to rule their territories. Not only that, but there is a term called "authorities". These are the rules, the laws. So in the case of America, our authority is the Constitution. It is the governing document by which the throne rules. But what we need to understand is that these units were created by God, but since administration was instituted after the "FALL', it is subject to the same Spiritual sicknesses as the rest of creation.

So what we must understand is: When sin entered the world, it corrupted not only human persons but also organizations. Therefore, Satan has his followers operating behind every human people. Friends? I asked God to disclose within me the works of the enemy., in these dangerous times, so that everyone can be helped! When you hear of evil people doing evil things through human institutions, those people are being manipulated like puppets on a string by a power outside themselves. But when good people do good things through human institutions, they reproduce the fact that Satan does not regulator every person in every position of authority. That's why evil people are still responsible for the evil they do, but what I want us to see is, there's a plan operating behind the throne. His name is Jesus! Let me give you an example.

"Dr. Martin Luther King, Jr." What was impressive about that movement is that it was generated and energized by involvement covered in prayer. Every time you looked up, whether it was a march of some other event, you saw people getting down on their knees to pray. "Obedience is better than sacrifice" !

Some years ago, a young woman from my church in "Compton California," came to my home crying because her boss was intentionally making her life miserable. He was resisting her even through she was fulfilling her responsibility under God on the job. Her boss had told her, "I'm going to make sure you don't get promotion. I don't like you. I don't like your Christianity. I don't like your morals. I'm going to make sure you go no where in this company." She came to me and said, "Evangelist Spencer, can you pray for me that God would intervene in this situation? We prayed for about a week, At the end of that time, she came in to see me all excited! I said, "What's going on? Did you find a new job?"

She said, "Let me tell you what Jesus did! When I went into work yesterday, my boss's office was cleaned out. His boss was dissatisfied with his work and fired him. And now I am promoted to his job." That was something I'll never forget. This young woman could have gone to war using the weapons of the flesh. She could have gotten ugly or become vindictive. But instead, she went to war in the heavenlies and there was a change in the power structure on earth. If all you see is the earthly conflict, you'll want to roll up your sleeves and fight. But when you understand the warfare in the heavenlies, it changes your approach.

This is exactly what the devil wants to do with the church. He wants to convince us that we are powerless and helpless so we will wind up being satisfied to be slaves. We'll be satisfied to have no victory in our lives, and before long we will be helping Satan out, building storage cities for Pharaoh. Unfortunately, the church has helped Satan out here by what I call a "theology of weakness." This is a religion that says the best we can hope to do is just get by. One reason so many believers are victimized by the theology of helplessness is that they can't distinguish what is from God and what is from Satan. They wind up resigning themselves to the wrong thing.

The Bible says We are to give thanks in everything. That does not say we have to give thanks in everything, For instance, 'if your loved one is dying' "[Like my husband, and my daughter)". I didn't say "thank you God that my loved one's is dying!" You say, "God, I thank you that You are in control of our circumstances and that You have promised to sustain us with Your love and grace no matter what happens." You don't have to give thanks for death because death is part of the cure. Its an enemy, a result of sin. We wouldn't know death if it were not for Satan and his rebellion. Death is his weapon. So in a hard circumstance like the death of a loved one, we have to distinguish between what is of God-grace, peace, strength and comfort-and what is of the devil-death and decay and the ruin of sin.

See, God's intent in any given situation is to build you up and strengthen you and make you more like Christ. Satan's intend in the same situation is to hurt you and tear you down and finally to destroy you. "God wants to HEAL you!" But the attacker wants to hurt you! "The doctor's intent in surgery is to fix and TREAT something that's wrong with you." So when the attacker; that is called Satan, comes to hurt you, No, you don't have to let Satan slice you up' you have been given "Powerful weapons" to resist him and tear down his strongholds! "Jesus Christ is your Healer indeed!"

Now, lets look at the "Message Accepting the Church's Assignment" Someday Jesus is going to come back physically and establish His worldwide rule. But until then, He wants us to wrestle against the principalities and powers! In other words, the Head of the church has done His part! He has deactivated Satan and given us all the power and spiritual authority we need! Now He wants His body to do its part, Which is to take His victory into every choice of human life an demonstrate His authority over it. This is why Paul prayed that we would know "the surpassing greatness of His power toward us who believe" [Ephesians 1:19]. This ought to raise a question in our minds. Why aren't the powers and rulers and territories of this earth identifying the authority of Christ?

There could be only one answer. The church is not doing its job! The body of Christ is not obeying its Head! Our assignment is to carry out what has been gifted by Christ on the cross by distributing all of God's truth to all the life. It is good for Christians to be involved in all of these activities. As I write this chapter, a member of our "District church in Los Angeles" has been elected "chairman of the school board". He is a godly man who has been bringing' God's kingdom agenda' to stand in the public scope for a long time. I applaud that.

Lastly, is the "Incredible Power Of Prayer"! Prayer engages the heavenlies. Paul understood that if you really want to see things change, the first person you have to talk to is God! If we want to see Satan's strongholds in the community come down, first of all, the church needs to go to prayer "for kings and all who are in authority." Do you want a more peaceful neighborhood? Do you want an environment of peace? The first thing to do, Paul says, is to carry those public officials to the throne of grace In prayer. We must pray for them because it is the people in authority who can influence and shape the quality of life for those in their area. But we are also to pray that those in authority might be saved.

"Prayer for those in authority is good and acceptable in the sight of God our Savior who desires all men to be saved, and to come to the knowledge of the truth" [1 Timothy 2: 3-4]. In other words, the church's prayer life should be so powerful that it helps to shape society. Could it be that we are not seeing more of God's movement in society because rather than praying first, the church is praying as a last option? If you want to pray with power for unsaved people, ask them if they have any needs you can pray for. Let them tell you when you pray for the needs of unbelievers in order to help them, and help lead them to Christ, God is motivated to act because He desires all people to be saved.

Notice that we must also come together in Jesus' name [Matthew 18:20]. This does not mean just closing our prayers" in Jesus' name. Amen." Jesus is not our errand boy. His name represents His authority. He must agree with what we are

his life, a spirit of fear tried to grab hold of him. That's why Paul told Timothy in Second Timothy 1:7 "For God hath not given us the spirit of fear; but of power, and of love, and of a sound mind." I want to especially point your emphasis to the words "sound mind." It suggests something that is delivered, revived, and protected and is now safe and secure. So, even if our mind is tempted to submit to fear, as was the case with Timothy, you can allow God's Word and the Holy Spirit to work in you to deliver, rescue, revive and salvage your mind. This means your emotions can be shielded from the unsoundly absurd, and crazy thoughts that have tried to grip your mind in the past, all you must do is grab hold of God's Word and His Spirit. You see, when your mind is guarded by the word of God, you think differently. When the Word of God is allowed to work in your mind, it protects your emotions: it defends your mind form demonic assault and it shields you from arrows the enemy may try to shoot in your direction in order to stimulate a spirit of fear inside you. Mildred's question is: Why, is it important for us to understand this? Because when you begin to live a life of faith; when you reach out to do the impossible, the enemy will try to attack you mentally and emotionally to stop your progress. For instance, he may speak to your mind, saying things like, you can't do this! This doesn't make sense! Are you crazy? In times like these, it is a blessing to know, "Angels Messages, to God Protects His People! Readers so, what do you do when the devil tries to convince you that you're losing your mind?

What do you do if you're confused due to stressful situations and so tempted to fear that you can't think straight? Go get alone with the Lord and give Him your concerns. As you focus on Jesus and release all those burdens, you'll find that your mind is working fine! [2nd Timothy 1'.7] promises you a sound mind; therefore, you have the right and privilege to tell the devil to shut up and then to declare by faith that your mind is sound, safe, and secure! Because the Holy Spirit is God! He is not just another spirit an angel; He is fully God, the sovereign third person of the Trinity. That means the angels are His messengers too. They act under His command. The Holy Spirit directs the angels in their ministry with and to God's people.

So, let's not confuse the Spirit's ministry with that of the angels. What a blessing to know that the Spirit was the Guide when Moses wrote, but the angels were involved in the delivery of God's law. In some way, under the Spirit's direction, the angels oversaw the transmission, protection, and integrity of the written Word. Therefore Mildred, want 'you all' to understand that "Christ is the head of every man, and the man is the head of every woman, and God is the head of Christ," So, now Paul goes into a discussion of praying and prophesying with and without head coverings. Please understand what I am saying, 'Whether this passage refers to a woman's long hair or to a covering over the hair is debated, Paul's plan was, woman should have her head covered when appealing in these activities, as a sign of her submission to God-ordained authority. In other words, the demons are promoting Satan's agenda through people they control. These may even be people who don't know they are being controlled by demons. I do believe; therefore, it is so important that you [not only) stay in tune spiritually yourself! But stay around people who are spiritually in tuned.

"I am tune in!" Because, I cannot dispute that a woman must wear 'hats' all the time. Why? because [l do not wear hats all the time]! Only when I want to wear hats!! However, I must agree with the "Word of God in [1 Corinthians 11:15) is saying, 'But if a woman has long hair, it is her glory? "For her hair is given to her for a covering!" Yet. This is what I have to say about the heads covering! 'l feel like, Christian women incline to "cover their head," to be both "comfortable and flattering," if you will! There is nothing wrong with that!

As l, traveled to various country's to Minister, it was imperative to have my head covered to Minister! Even ladies, that are in the congregation! But, I have never gone against their instructions and guidelines, I respect them, because I was there for one reason! 'To Preach the Word of God," that lives might be saved and changed!" To the "(Officials and Leaders abroad)", I pray God's blessing upon you!" That's why, it didn't matter to me about the covering, because, I live in the [Untied States of America] ! That's means, in my state, I do not have to preach with my head covered, unless it was ordered by: "The Church officials," for certain occasions! Every country has its own instructions!

Therefore, the Bible tells us to "test the spirits." The first and most important test is found in [John 4: verses 2-23]. Let me show you something here, Elisha's servant wanted to get practical. "What are we going to do"? Watch out for Christians who always want to be practical. You need to hang around Christians who want to be supernatural, not just practical. So, "Angels Messages to God, protects His people." Christians who live supernaturally can look beyond what is visible. They understand that they are in a spiritual battle, so they aren't limited by what they see around them. Maybe they can see God's solution.

I believe people's attitude ought to be, "Lord, if there's something I'm not seeing, show me, so that I won't react just to what I see -the enemies. But I'll react to what you are doing. Ask God to open your eyes! We saw in [Acts 12] that an angel delivered Peter from prison. But this was the second time this had happened to Peter. Earlier, the high priest and his pals put all the apostles in prison.

Here's another way God delivers His protection to us through the angels. In the middle of the story about the rich man and Lazarus, Jesus said this about the death of Lazarus: "It came about the poor man died and he was carried away by the angels to Abraham's bosom". The angel transported Lazarus to heaven. Why would Lazarus need an angelic escort into the heavenly realm? To get from earth to heaven, I feel like he had to pass through the enemy territory. Friends, if hell had its way, it would never let [you or l] out of that grave to get to heaven. I was talking about heaven, sometimes ago, I was talking to a "friend Pastor", about how people mess around with Satan, because that enemy is sneaky!

But we don't have to worry about hell winning, even after you diel because God will give His angels the message to escort us to glory! We will be protected and escorted through the enemy territory into heaven and the presence of God. With protection! Look at Psalm 78, "The psalmist refers to the manner that God rained down on the people". Then read this statement: "Man did eat the bread of angels" [V. 25]. Readers? Can you imagine that Manna was basically cornflakes from above? I'm talking about little white flakes that rained down from heaven to supernaturally supply the people's need. This is what God did, He told the angels to deliver food to the Israelites. They were the messengers of His provision. A lot of times when God answers our prayers, we think the answer just showed up. No, it was delivered by God's carriers, His angels.

Let me clarify something. I do not mean to suggest that you and I can force the angelic world to do anything we want. The angels obey their "Boss", Our authority comes from our relationship with God through Jesus Christ. What the psalmist is saying that the plagues of Egypt were caused by angels. They are actively engaged in spiritual warfare today,

This story is important for our purposes because in it Jesus reveals a truth about the work of angels that we need to understand and appropriate for our lives today. Nathaniel was taken back by this and asked Jesus how He knew him. Jesus revealed to Nathaniel that He had seen him earlier when he was sitting under a fig tree before Nathaniel ever thought about coming to see Jesus. After all that had happened, Jesus was saying something important but himself, and the ministry of angels, and it wasn't just for Nathaniel. It's for all of God's people.

In the year of 2017, I put some food in the over to cook. While it was cooking, I laid down on the couch, in the living room. Unfortunately, I fell asleep, and can still remember lying there and almost hearing a voice inside of me saying, "Get up. Get up." I turned over tried to ignore the feeling. But it got louder: "Get up!" "Get up!" So, I jumped up, wondering was going on in the house, it was so Smokey! Then I remembered; food was in the oven. I ran to the kitchen, and flames of fire was rising over the stove! Then I realized how serious this fire is!

My son "Nathaniel, and my son-in-law, Pastor Richardson, happens to be here in their rooms, at such a time as this! They tried everything to put the fire outl In the meantime, I call (911)! Because of a "Secret Servicemen, wife," there were so many "fireman, and officers here! After they were finish with everything, I asked all of them to please hold hands, and "1 prayed for God's protection upon their lives!" it was such joy seeing them-taking of their hats an received prayer! I firmly believe that this incident was an example of "angelic activity in my life as a child of God!" it was "My guardian angels" Because "Angels, Messages to God, protects his people!"

Many of you, may have had similar stories of being "touched by an angel" in your own life as well! Maybe, it was a time you were nodding off behind the wheel of your car, and suddenly awaken, just in time to steer away from a disaster! As we begin our second section, which will deal with God's holy angels, it's time to restate foundational thesis of this book. The physical, visible realm is greatly affected by the spiritual, invisible realm that the Bible calls the heavenly places.

What happens in the spiritual realm controls and influences what happens in the visible spiritual realm. So, the better we understand the invisible spiritual realm, the more prepared we will be to wage successful spiritual warfare against our adversary the devil. Where were the angels created? The Bible gives us a clue in Job 38, "The morning stars" are the angels! It is a real blessing to know that "Angels, Messages to God, protects His people." Since that's the case, Satan will be conquered'!

I want to close this chapter with an amazing biblical account that puts some "skin" on it's matter of conquering Satan. The story is found in Zechariah 3. In a vision the prophet Zechariah saw Joshua, the high priest of this day, saying before the angel of the Lord, and Satan standing at his right hand to accuse him"! So Satan came to be Joshua's challenger, to prosecute him before Jesus. It doesn't say Jesus was here, but "the angel of the Lord" In the Old testament is a reference to Jesus in His eternal divinity, before He came to earth. But thanks be to God, when you met Jesus, He will set you free from Satan's kingdom.

I believe that the elements of nature such as thunder and lightning are sometimes manifestations of God's angels. Let illustrate what I mean. When I was in Boston, MA, every weekend I would go to visit my cousin who lived on a nearby street. I would be sitting, watching television, and sometimes it would start to thunder, and lighting would flash, then the rain would come down heavy! My cousin said tome, Mildred, turn off the television!" I wanted to know why? Her answer was, "Because God is talking." and we need to pay attention.

She may not have had the application of Scripture exactly right, but the principle behind her conviction is solidly biblical. The prophet, in Ezekiel 1, said, in effect, "I saw the wind. And when my eyes were opened, and I was able to look inside the wind, and I saw "Angeles moving there." Let me establish this concept further with this extended quote from Psalm 18, a glorious statement about the power of angels. Don't go looking for angels; go looking for Jesus. Don't go looking for guardian angel. He has already found you. Go looking for Jesus. Angels are God's ministering servants, but when it comes to Jesus, God the Father says, "O God." Only Jesus is the Son of God. Only Jesus is God Himself, the second person of the Trinity. Jesus is the name to know.

CHAPTER 8

"What Do I Do When I Don't Know What To Do?"

Do you ever feel like you're going in circles and not making any progress? At least not the kind of progress you were expecting. If you're like "Me", there is a plan and dream you would want to fulfill. That plain is, we must understand that life is confusing at times. And most days it seems like we are just surviving instead of live-in out those dreams of accomplishing goals. There have been days I've felt like one foot was fixed to the floor, while my other foot was directed in another direction. Can you relate?

To many times I've second guessed about a decision I was confident about. I wanted so desperately to follow God's will; but then I felt uncertain not wanting to make a wrong move. When things like this accrue, it's time to stop and pray! As I was wrestled with indecision and insecurity, I've sought God's word for help. then I felt in my Spirit, this is not what I am supposed to be doing. When we Pray and read the Word Of God, it addresses our desires for guidance and shows us "what to do, and what not to do!" As I was studying [Psalm 25:4-51],

These verses reveal David's humble and teachable heart! He wanted to be guided by God and led by His truth. David knew "God was his Savior," and placed all his hope in the One that created the right path for him. "My message is; you must trust God when you don't know what to do!"

Although it may be possible to run a church, business, or organization singlehandedly, it is certainly not the most efficient or effective method of operation. Nevertheless, countless people have tried to do so with small success. Expected, however these same people eventually get so tired that they just can't run the whole show anymore, After a while, even the most committed become weary of carrying never -ending responsibility alone. Doing things alone is a course of action that guaranties your project will never be large, You may do a top-quality job that touches a very small market, but your lack of a team restricts your ability to touch very many people at one time. You can run the operation singlehandedly on a small scale, but you won't be able to have a large church, business, or organization without the empower needed to touch and serve many people.

"The attitude of doing it all single hand, limits the growth of any body, not to mention the fact that it can physically wear you out and make you "old at an early age!" Thanks be to God, I am "eighty years old" now but I will always look attractive, because of "God's Grace and Mercy!" That's why Paul compared the Church to the human body, with different parts that are armed to perform different functions. He says, "For as the body is one, and hath many members, and all the members off that one body, being many, are one body: also, is Christ." As believes we must say goodbye to our old, self-governing way of thinking and learn how to be united into a greater whole. We need each other for without each other's input and gifts, we are incomplete.

When God's people come together as a team to achieve a common goal, their unified effort brings divine power and world transforming moves of God to the earth! Doctrine, culture, language, and creeds will never bring unity to the Church. But when we become single focused, working together as a team to win the world to Jesus Christ, that is when genuine unity will come to the Church. And unity is such a powerful force! For some, unit is an unclear dream like wish for a day when Christians sweetly smile at each other and sing in harmony. Disagreements are resolved and eliminated; and we all say thanks and do the same identical things. But the Bible never promises that a day will come when we all agree about everything! This is a false concept of unity. It's imaginary that will never be reached on this earth. Say, "Lord What Do I Do When I Don't Know?"

So, what is unity? Unity occurs when people are united In action and in passion for common cause. Their shared goal is so strong that it removes hostilities, puts away disagreements, and gives previously divided people a reason to take their place alongside each other. When this occurs, different gifts, talents, and anointings become connected together, and the result is an amazing river of gifts, talents, and anointings become connected together, and the result is an amazing river of divine power that achieves the supernatural and accomplishes the impossible. I can tell you that in our "Pastors Ministry," organization leadership team is very gifted; and holy! Yet we are extremely united as a ministry. It is our common goal to get the Gospel to as many people as we can by God's grace, This single purpose pulls our whole diverse staff together in extraordinary unity, which is one of the reasons we have had such powerful results. We may be many in number and diverse in gifts and talents, but we are one in purpose.

When you get discouraged and are tempted to give up; when times are rough and your faith isn't finding its fulfillment as quickly as you desire; you must decide to put everything on hold. Tell your mind to be silent: command your emotions to be stilled; and remember, when you were first illuminated to the truth of God's Word.: To say; "What To Do When I Don't Know?" I have no doubt as to what God has celled me to do with my life. He has called me to "Preach the Gospel," and to help establish the Church In regions of the world" that are unstable.

Many of them are difficult, and unchurched! "This is my calling" and I am very confident of this fact! When you look at the life of the "Apostle Paul," it talk's about the Power of teamwork. This will help you to understand how to "Do what You Don't Know What to Do!" It is simply a fact that is given to building this kind of teamwork. People who become covered together by a common goal produce unity. And when this kind of interaction is at work among your team members in your Church Ministry business, or organization, that team becomes a mighty force that helps you reach the goals and visions God has placed in your heart.

So, don't try to fulfill your dream or run your church, ministry, business, or organization singlehandedly. If you do you'll only serve to bodily, emotionally, and spiritually exhaust yourself. Why don't you instead allow God to bring another team members to you who can help you fulfill your task? Don't settle for accomplishing your goal single handedly on a small scale. Develop the manpower in business, or organization with enough hands to touch and serve any people in your department! As other members join your team and begin to use their gifts and talents to press toward the common goal, you'll find that their help greatly enhances both your effectiveness and your ability to impact this world for God. So why don't you ask God today to bring you the individuals you need to help you fulfill your God given assignment? Such as the ushers, Deacons, missionary s Evangelism. etc, What Do You Do When You Don't Know?

But the question I'm asking is, what amazing idea has God called you and l, to do, that goes beyond the basics of living a godly life? And will we step out in Faith and do it, even if it's outside our comfort zone? No! We must be led by the 'Holy Spirit'. What doors dose God want us to walk through? What opportunities have been placed in our path for us to developed as disciples of Christ and as leaders? What need could we be fulfilling that we see in our local Churches and communities? What idea has God put in our heart and mind that we must share!

I really believe we are called for a greater purpose that just existence. I believe God has given each of us many similar and different talents that He wants us to develop and use to help not only each other, but also those we encounter in our day-to-day lives', no question. We have such a tremendous opportunity every day to do well and be a special godly light; to be a "different kind of beat for the world to hear!" This amazing thing God wants you to do might not be a 'global movement' and millions of lives, but it might have a huge impact in a few lives! And wouldn't that be worth it? Also, worth you listening to that still small voice stepping up to the plate!

So, if you are like me and you are wondering how to figure out what God want us to do, let me suggest that we first get on our "knees and pray" that 'God's Spirit' be burnt in each of us to have the attitude of Christ when its comer to serving. That is why service motivated by love and compassion for others is a pure reflection of the same attitude that Christ had and has for everyone to this day!

Nest, we need to open our eyes. What do I mean by that? There are needs within our church and communities that we can quit frankly close our eyes to, and believe that if we don't see it, then it's not really a problem. How untrue is that statement? If you and I see a need with our eyes, I believe it becomes our responsibility to see it filled! Whether that be 'offering kind words, and moments of your life' to a person you visibly see that has a "sad countenance", offering a meal or snack to someone who you see that looks hungry: mentoring a young boy or girl, in your local church or community who's life not have the best influence at home; 'speaking or writing edifying words for others to hear and to read; holding up the weak so others can increase.

When my family and I first move to [Sunny mead, California, before it was call the city of "[Moreno Valley California]. God connected us to some of the most wonderful, loving people to be known. Although, some of them were from different cultures, they were sincere! They became some outstanding people toward our family! I believe we should

"Be affectionate to one another!" This was a blessing for our family! We discovered a level of relationship in the Christian community. Also, I can never forget "Pastor and Lady Bell," Also both, the late Pastor and Lady Franking Knight." With much symphony!"

My opinion is: unfortunately, in many parts of the Christian community, this level of relationship I have described; is sadly absent! In these days all over the state, it is unhappy to see that people attending church weekly; and hardly know the people they frequently sit next to in church services. Life has become so busy with natural concerns that most believers suffer from a "severe deficiency" of relationships with their fellow believers. This was never God's plan for the [local Church]. For He designed it to be a place where people's lives could be built together as living stones. His plan was and still is to have a people who demonstrates 'His covenant nature' in their relationships with one another.

I guest in a way our question is answered. What does God want us to do? One thing is to serve, even if it might be awkward. And if you look at the men and women of character in the Bible, that's what they did.

That's what they devoted their lives to! Let me implore everyone who reads this to step up and be leaders who God has in store for you to do! Go and be a servant of the living God and find the needs that are not being met and meet them! Behold, be courageous, and humbly ask God, "Lord, What Do You Want Me to Do, When I Don't Know What to Do?

CHAPTER 9

"It's Time To Make A Change In Our Situation"

Your biggest potential enemy in life besides your own wrong thinking and the devil himself is the environment in which you live. For instance, if you constantly live in an atmosphere of doubt and unbelief, it's just a fact that you'll have a much more difficult time maintaining a walk of strong faith. That doubt-filled environment will try to rub off on you!

It's just a fact that your situation tends to affect you and the way you think. For example, if you used to smoke or if you used to have a drinking problem, it's obviously not a smart idea for you to hang around smokers or drinkers unless, that is, you want to be influenced to return to your old habits. Hanging around people who will do these things may trap you to pick up a cigarette to take a smoke or to allow yourself one more small drink. However, those little endowments may possibly be the very hook that the devil uses to drag you back into the bondage from which Jesus Christ already delivered you. That's why it's vital for you to understand that the environment surrounding you is very important! Look at the phrase "the sin which doth so easily beset you."

Sometimes to make necessary changes in your live, you must physically remove yourself from an inefficient situation.

If you're not strong enough in your faith to stay there without being affected, you need to get up and get out of that unbelieving, negative situation. The one you've been comfortable living in for a long, long time. If you're not strong enough to overcome it, it will undeniably try to reach out and drag you back into your old behavior again.

If God's warning to lay aside every weight applies to you, then obey Him and make a break from that unhealthy situation! Perhaps old friends, old places, or wrong believing are trying to apply a bad influence on you and you're not resisting that influence too well. If that's the case, get out of there! For you, that environment is sin if it keeps you from fulfilling your potential in Jesus Christ. Be honest as you consider your workplace, your friends, and your living conditions. Ask yourself, is this situation conductive to my walk in Christ or is it dragging me back down into the mud I was delivered from? Your friends and your job are not so important that you should let them destroy your spiritual life. If you cannot successfully handle the situation you're in, get out of there. Then watch the Lord do a better job and better friends than you've ever had in your life!

"It's Time to Make a Change in our Situation!" The reason being, is that Satan didn't want to pray, "Thy Kingdom come, thy will be done." He wanted to be managing their kingdom. 'Readers', you must agree with Mildred, that the battle is not ours, it belongs to the Lord. Then Satan said, "I will ascend above the heights of the clouds, you see as you fly in an airplane. Many people have ascended above the clouds in airplanes. There's more to this declaration than that. As I understand the revelation of God's Word, the Bible associate's clouds with the glory of God [Exodus 16:10; 40:34]. His glory often appeared as a cloud, So, the clouds are those things through which the glory of God is manifested.

Satan wanted glory. He wanted praise. He tempted Jesus by showing Him the kingdom of the world and saying "All these things will I give You if You fall down to worship me" [Matthew 4:9]. Satan wanted to be worshipped! When Mildred read this, I said "Oh No, Satan!" That's why Satan cannot hang out with You and l, when we are worshipping God. He can't stand it because we are giving God that which He so desperately wants for himself.

Not only that but when worshiping God, it reminds Satan of what he used to do! He used to bring God glory. But then Satan tried to share what can't be shared. He wanted to divide something that is indivisible, the glory of God.

But, "It's Time to Make a Change in Our Situation!" The reason you and I can't get stuck on ourselves is that there is always somebody better than us, prettier than us, smarter than us. Better at business than us. But God is Himself. There is no one like Him nor will there ever be anyone like Him. So, he will share His glory with none of His creatures. So, lets hold on to God's statement!

Because now, this is really the statement of a fool. Here is Satan, looking up at the all-knowing, all-powerful, all-present God and saying, "I'm going to be like Him." We all know, for Satan to be like God would mean there would be two Gods!

But that isn't going to happen. God says, "Before Me, there was no God formed, and there will be none after Me" [Isaiah 43:10]. When Satan said he was going to become like God, he was saying he wanted the independence God has.

God is totally independent. He is answerable to no one outside of Himself. And God is all-knowing. Satan tempted Eve by saying that if she ate the fruit, she would have knowledge like God' [genesis 3:51]. You and I can say somebody tempted us. That doesn't exonerate us by at least we didn't come up with the sins we commit all on our own. But Satan had no outside pressure. He wasn't fighting a spiritual battle against a clever enemy. He rebelled on his own.

So, let me just say here, that one reason God permitted Satan's rebellion was to show the angels and us that when we don't live life His way, it doesn't work. Satan was determined to do it his way, and God let him do it his way. Let me say, "It's Time to Make a Change In Our Situation!" let 'Mildred' put it another way. As Satan learned, even when you sin, you sin according to God's rules, not yours. Satan would come to understand that he was not just the devil; he was the devil under God's absolute control. We know that the mountain of God has to do with His throne, the place from which He rules. So, Satan lost his privileged place near God's throne. He still has access to God's presence, as Job I reveals. "But now he can only come to God as a visitor," Satan has no place in heaven anymore.

Therefore, Faith connects between rebellion and Spiritual Warfare. What we have been talking about is opening to the reality known as Spiritual Warfare. The first thing we need to understand is that when God permits Satan's sin. And then judged him and his rebellious angels, He did more than just pronounce their curse. So, God said to Satan, "l am going to show you something. I am going to demonstrate to you and to the angelic world My power and glory. I am going to unfold before your eyes a plan that will demonstrate I am not to be played with." So, Satan was expelled from heaven and reduced to the earth realm.

This is where things get interesting; because warfare really began. ""The earth was 'formless and void', and darkness was over the surface of the deep." "Mildred is going to put it another way", the earth was a garbage dump, a wasteland. Everything was sort of floating together in a formless mass. I call it a "swamp in the country, like a place where I was born." Later God had to separate the water from the dry land. The point is that wherever Satan resides, wherever he's in control, he creates disorder and garbage. That's why when Adam and Eve yielded to Satan, they were kicked out of Eden.

Now let me show you what happened when God began to create. God asks Job where he was when God created the earth. God says when the angels saw His creative power, they "sang together" [Job 38:7]. Here then is the connection between Satan's rebellion and spiritual warfare. That smaller creature was mankind, you and me. God was saying to Satan, "l can take a creature of less beauty and ability than you, but who trusts Me, and I will do more with this weaker creature than you can do with all of your power." That' why we must be led by the Holy Spirit."

It may be hard for you to believe, but most of what we have done in life has been initiated by us, not by the spirit of God. After the ball is rolling and we've already starred "doing our thing," that's usually when we pray and ask God to bless what we have initiated. We just assume that it is His will because it seems like such a good idea. No wonder we have such poor results! We must learn to put on the brakes, stop ourselves for a while, and learn to wait until the Holy Spirit speaks clearly to our hearts. It may seem as if this way of doing things takes longer. The Holy Spirit speaks clearly tour hearts.

It may seem as if this way of doing things takes longer; but when He does speak, the results will be more rewarding and longer lasting. Furthermore, we can avoid pit-falls that would have cost us a lot of time and effort in the long run.

Believers must learn to let the Holy Spirit lead them. Take healing as an example. How many ministers have thought, I'm going to empty all those wheelchairs by praying for those sick people! But after they finished praying most of the people were still in their wheelchairs and those ministers left feeling uncomfortable, defeated, and powerless. Didn't God want to heal those people? Of course, He did, but the anointing may not have ben present at that exact moment to heal in that way.

Being sensitive to the Holy Spirit is important if we want to see successful results in any scope of life, including healing, family, business, and leading a church congregation. Only the Holy spirit sees and knows everything that should be done; that's why it is so imperative to learn how to follow His leadership if we want to be successful in life. I think a classic example of being led by the Spirits be seen in the account of the two blind beggars in Matthew 9:27-31. These two blind beggars heard that Jesus was walking by so that they waited for Him to heal them. However, Jesus walked right past, never stopping to heal them. The two blind beggars were so upset that when Jesus departed forward, two blind men followed him, crying, and saying, "Thou son of David, have mercy on us."

Even though these two men were blind and couldn't continue to tell us that they were "crying' out. In other words, they were screaming as loudly as possible to get Jesus' attention! What a dramatic picture! Think about it! They were shouting, and yelling, trying to get Jesus to notice them. But He just continued walking on as though they weren't even there. Following Jesus persistently, they hunted along in their darkness, still screaming, yelling, and crying out for Him to heal them. Finally, Jesus came to the two blind beggars and asked, "Do you believe that I am able to do this?" They answered" Yea, Lord." "Then He touched their eyes saying, according to your faith be it unto you. "But why didn't Jesus stop and heal the blind men when He first saw them?

Why didn't He immediately turn to heal them when He recognized their blind condition? And why did He answer them, "According to your faith be it unto you"? I'll tell you why? "It Was time to Make a change in their Situation!" Jesus evidently did not sense the anointing to heal at that moment; otherwise, He would have stopped to lay His hands on those men. However, this didn't stop the two blind men from receiving. It was as though Jesus said, "l don't sense the anointing to heal right now so you're going to have to receive this on your own!

Be it unto you according to your faith !"

So, the only explanation for the fact that Jesus didn't stop to heal the two blind beggars is that the Holy Spirit wasn't leading Him to heal at that exact moment. The good news is that the two blind men could use their own faith to be healed anyway, and they were healed! As for those whom the Holy Spirit led Jesus to heal, He healed them with a perfect-percentage. The Bible describes His healing ministry this way: "And the whole multitude sought to touch him: for there were virtue out of him and, healed them all" [Like 5:179. You see, when that healing virtue was flowing, everyone got healed. But when it wasn't flowing, Jesus didn't attempt to heal. That's why, "It's time to make a change in our salutation". So, be aware of hands' being laid on a person to receive healing! We must realize that it is the "flowing off the anointing', with the "Power of the' Holy Ghost' in your "hands," for the Lord to heal and deliver some one! In other instances, like Luke 5:17 where Jesus was busy teaching the Word of God Suddenly He sensed that "the power off the Lord was present to heal them."

When Jesus sensed the anointing to heal, He put aside His teaching and followed the leading of the Spirit. As a result, multitudes were healed that day, including the paralytic that a group of friends lowered down to the room through an opening in the roof of the house. "l must pause here and say", I am thankful, because I remember my father, A pastor told his best friend about my calling to the Field. He lived in Georgia. And for a long time now he is diseased! At that time, he was a "Retried Apostle in the Gospel!" he was on the field around the world. This Apostle took time to instruct an informed me, since I was called to the field, the "different between "field and locally preaching!" I listen, I took notes, and I also followed instructions; according to what God would tell me do!

I well understand that; field work or, local work' is not your choice to do what self tells you to do! But, to make sure; it is the moving of 'God's anointing' before laying your hands on a person! also, make sure it is God's Word, before giving "A prophecy"! Prophecy is not what we think, or already know! An I understand that!

That's why I love this example in Like 5:7, for it shows Jesus' flexibility in the hands of the Holy Spirit. Although He Was busy teaching now, suddenly He felt the anointing shift. The Power of God was suddenly present to heal the sick, and Jesus knew it was time to set aside the preplanned program and go with the flow of the Holy Spirit. My readers, this is what 'The Author is talking about! Jesus faithfully followed wherever the Holy Spirit led, and He did what the Holy Spirit told Him to do. If the spirit told Him nothing, then nothing was the right thing for Him to do. However, I have experience hard work, unexpected living! Also eating in different countries! But thank God for His protection in my life!

Jesus told the disciples, "l can of mine own self do nothing; "as I hear, I judge: and my judgment is just, "Notice that Jesus said" as I hear, I judge," You see, Jesus was constantly listening to the voice of the Spirit, waiting for that divine signal to act, to heal, to deliver, or to cleanse someone who was sick. Then Jesus said what He did as soon as He was confident of the Spirit's direction to act." This word is used in John 5:30 to let us know that Jesus never acted until He had all the direction he needed from the Spirit. Once that direction was given, and Jesus had all the information He needed, He acted. Because He acted on directions given by the Spirit of God If we will listen to the Spirit and do what He tells us to do, if we will learn to wait until we hear Him speak, we will have powerful results just like Jesus had in His earthly ministry! So, what about you, friend? are you ready to let the Holy Spirit become the Leader in your life today?

Let me give you a few more reasons that God permitted Satan to rebel and then judged him. God wanted to show His hatred of sin and His justice. He wants us to see through all this that He is a holy and perfect God who judges sin. God also wanted to reveal His wisdom. Paul said that God does what He does so that His "diverse wisdom" of His plan of redemption. So God wanted to show them the glory of His grace when it is received by repentant sinners.

If you want to correct the effects of Satan's rebellion in your life, you must learn that God will go to huge lengths to guard and preserve His glory. God will spare nothing to preserve His glory. To all my readers, if you try to interfere with God's glory, and try to take from God that which belongs to Him alone, you are in trouble. A lot of people in the Bible had to learn that lesson the hard way as well The Bible tells us to humble ourselves before God. "Your Author" wants to clarify right here! Humbling yourself does not mean that you go around saying, "Poor me, I'm nothing. I'm never going to be anything." That's not true humility. True humility is gaging yourself against he right standard and knowing where you stand in relation to that standard.

"Please Listen to this story if you will!" A little boy came to his father one day and said, "Dad, I measured myself, and I'm eight feet, four inches tall." His father said, "Son, you know you're not eight feels tall." The boy said, "yes, I am," he said, "l measured myself, and I'm more than (eight rulers tall)." The father went to see what the boy was measuring himself with! A lot of us think more of ourselves than we ought to think, because we're measuring ourselves against the wrong people. We're comparing ourselves with each other instead of normal, which the bible says is the "glory of God" [Romans 3:2321. Pride was Satan's sin and it will bring us down quickly. Here is the "Author's prayer for you!"

"Lord, I want to learn how to follow You closely! To learn the sound of Your voice, when You are speaking to me, to lead me, to become sensitive to You that know when to act and when to wait. I am sorry for all the times I've acted before praying, I don't want to function this way anymore. I want to know what You are instructing me to do. Give me boldness to wait!" (l Pray this in Jesus' Name)!"

"IT'S TIME TO MAKE A CHANGE
IN OUR SITUATION!"

CHAPTER 10

"Women Are Motivated To Be Creative"

During my life time, so many women and men have approached me saying, "Mildred, your life is so inspired!" I am feeling the same way, about many of you women, as well! As I looked over the distance as the sun was sitting, I pictured the creator of the manufacture. A creator of all humankind and a creator who can shaped your character in his own image. It is an honor to know women of worth, moral, uprightness and honesty in character. The character of a virtuous woman is of self-respect. Many women desiring to be creative, have not discovered the deep truths of the word of God and do not know how to apply the word to their lives; they are still searching for identity in Christ Jesus. They are frustrated and puzzled because they do not know the path to wholeness in Christ Jesus.

Do you know your individuality or your mark of identity? The "Creative woman of God" is a woman of shaped difference. This woman has an identified character and is acquainted with the way she wishes to attain. She allows God to mold and shape her purpose. As you look into the mirror of the Word of God, you will begin to recognize the personality of God and detention of his likeness.

As you set before God in devotion, study, and meditation of the word each day with the enthusiasm of these women that will reveal to you the awesomeness of God and his mighty power in transforming the character of women. You will begin to sup with the Lord and realize the potential that the "Creative woman" has, and the reward one can obtain if they continue to be steadfast, unmovable, and always abounding in the work of the Lord. "Creative woman" of God, strived to be all that you can be in the Lord. Be fruitful, creative, and productive in abundance, and you will influence the lives of others in a remarkable way. Desire the sincere milk of the Word so that you may be able to impart into others the beauty of our Lord and Savior Jesus Christ. Walk according to the Word of God and receive your honorable and righteous position in Christ,

Ladies, may I share with you the incredible things about "Mildred" in my Christian walk as a woman of God? I have met many challenges and obstacles as I endeavored to submit myself to the will of God. I realized early in my Christian walk that I must study the Word of God, ask for what I desired in life, and then apply the Word to my life that is, not just read the Word, but study the Word and seek the face of God in guidance. Make sure your foundation in life is built on the Word of God.

Many woman of God are not growing in ministry for many reasons. The cares of this world can hinder you from walking in the newness of Christ. God's will for man is to live a life that is joyful, peaceable, and totally surrendered to His will. When you become a new creature in Christ, you are delivered from the cares of the world and walk in newness of the spirit. You are transformed, which means that your life has change and you walk according to the instructions given in the Word of God. You must now walk as a holy vessel putting away bitterness, malice, uncleanliness, hatred, jealousy, envy and all the things that are contrary to God's Word. Old ways will pass away and all things become new.

I petitioned the Lord for deliverance and freedom in all areas for my life and for the life of women in ministry. My heart was heavy because I could not understand why Christians struggle with each other being that, we are on the same holy team. I resolved within that we are sitting among believers in the fellowship of the brethren and yet held in bondage. We are in bondage because of lack of knowledge. We are killing one another to satisfy our own personal desires. We are not just haters, but murderers. In the stillness of the night, God whispered and said to me," Whom the Father has set free is free indeed." As believers, we have been set free. We are no longer under the bondage of the world. We no longer walk as the world does, but as new creatures in Christ Jesus Yes, I desire to share with women throughout the world the love and compassion of God through ministering exhortating inspiration, and deliverance. Women of God, you can be free. ":Creative Women" of God, you can go forth in victory and in the power of the Holy Ghost. Be strong and courageous, for victory is yours. Study God's Word and submit to the will of God, then endure until the end and you will have victory and eternal life with Christ Jesus.

so now lets talk about "WOMAN STRIVING TO BE FRUITFUL!" As we all know, many women of God are being held hostage by the enemy while standing on holy grounds. Christian women's hearts are longing to serve God with a passion desire to be use by God, but because of lack of knowledge, many are held hostage as the enemy of God. Woman of God, be subject one to another. Humble yourselves therefore under the mighty hand of God that he may exalt you in due time. First peter [4:11 states, "For as much then as Christ hath suffered for us in the flesh, arm yourselves likewise with the same mind: for he that hath suffered in the flesh hath ceased from sin." Walk in love among ourselves.

And You will inherit the blessings of the Lord if you be all of one mind, having compassion one of another, loving the brothern, be graceful, be courteous: Do not "render evil for evil, or hedge for hedge: but blessing; knowing that ye are there called, that ye should inherit a blessing'. First Peter [3:14-15] says, But and if ye suffer for righteousness sake, happy are ye: and be not afraid of their terror, neither be troubled; But sanctify the Lord God in your hearts: and be ready always to give an answer to every man that asketh you a reason of the hope that is in you with meekness and fear."

Through patience and prayer, sanctify yourself; seek God's guidance in your daily life. Worship the Lord in the spirit of humility. Allow him to clean your heart from the sin that hiders you from obeying his commands, and you will become "Fruitful women of God" you must remember that, "fruitful woman is a woman of many divisions." But this woman strives to serve and be a witness of God. Her heart longs for God and her desire is to see shackles loosed, handcuffs destroyed, and deliverance takes place in God's people.

She is a wise woman who is smart and clever in her perception of life. She is very intelligent and balanced, yet she can be held hostage amount supporters. She recognizes areas in her life where she needs liberation. Some of these areas are viewed as untouchable, but her decision is to enter into that territory and destroy the shackle and bondage. This woman is a woman of power, for she weighs all matters and reveals authority and control with great influence. She is a woman of character, for her makeup and disposition is one of honest grit. A woman of virtue for she has necessary qualities and features. She typifies good values and good worth and has merits. She is a woman of self-assurance, for she is confident and has great self-respect. A woman of abundance and wealth for plenty is one of her great qualities. A woman of contentment, for she is happy and has pleasure and satisfaction in serving God and others. Moreover, a woman of creativity for she has great creativity and mind, which is inventive in her vision for life and ministry.

All women have a need for love, appreciation, respect, and admiration. But at some time in our life, you have those who are not pleasant; however, they are place in your surroundings for you to minister wholeness and help to develop positive character in their lives. The "Fruitful woman" is a doer of the Word and practices a lifestyle that is pleasing to God and not one that is selfish.

Woman of God, make sure that your life is rich with properties that do not gratify the flesh but properties that give glory and honor to our Lord and Savior, Jesus Christ.

Psalms 111:10 says, "The fear of the Lord is the beginning of wisdom: a good understanding have all they that do his commandments: his praise endureth for ever." Over come fear through the study and application of God's Word, demonstrate the gifts of God in your daily devotion before Him and remember that the foundation of our life is the inner beauty of the Word of God. That word stood out in my spirit!

Therefore, I started searching about "Women of beauty". [Psalms 149:4]; that scripture says: "For the Lord aketh pleasure in his people: he will beautify the meek with salvation" it's amazing how God can direct a child of God to see and, take notice what His Word is about!

"Woman Of Beauty," seeks to beautify the heart through the teachings of God. The teaching and principles of God will build a solid foundation for your Christian walk. Seek wisdom, knowledge, and understanding of God's Word, for this will guide you and instruct you in his ways and prepare you for effective ministry.

When you minister before the people of God, wisdom, knowledge, and understanding of his Word should be your foundation in order to bring deliverance and freedom to the people. Seek God in all matters of life and keep wisdom as a treasure. Knowledge and understanding of God is your illumination to know the hope of his calling and the riches of the glory of his inheritance in all believers. Be a wise woman desiring to please God by doing the will of God. Stay before God and allow him to teach you his ways. We are new creatures and should walk according to the newness in Christ in order to have peace and mercy in our lives. This newness in Christ enlightens our heart so we may know the hope we have in Him.

Woman of God, saturate yourself in God's Word so that you will grow and mature in the wisdom and knowledge of Christ Jesus. Live a meek and humble life in the spirit of humility before God. Preach and teach the good tidings of the Lord. Isaiah 52:7 states, "how beautiful upon the mountains are the feet of him that bringeth good tidings, that publisheth peace; that bringeth good tidings of good, that publisheth peace; that bringeth good tidings of good, that publisheth salvation; that saith unto Zion, Thy God reigneth!" The Lord takes pleasure in his people and will beautify the meek with salvation. woman of God, reflect your inner beauty by beholding the beauty of the living and true God. It is a blessing to completes the "walks of life." Look at Ecclesiastes 12:13. I read about a Missionary was preaching in the village market, and some of the people were laughing at her because she was not a very beautiful woman. She took it for a time, and then she said to the crowd, "It is true that I do not have beautiful hair, for I am almost bald. Nor do I have beautiful teeth, for they are really not mine; they were made by the dentist. I do not have a beautiful face, nor can I afford to wear beautiful clothes. But this I know: I have beautiful feet!" And she quoted the verse from Isaiah: "How beautiful upon the mountains are the feet of them that bringeth good tidings.

With every thing that's happening in the lives of men and women, there must be an example of "keeping a good relationship." I can remember, some time ago, I sat in a church and watched a young bride and groom pledge their love. It was a beautiful occasion, with a handsome groom, a lovely bride, and many will-wishers gathered to witness their vows and celebrate their happiness. But would it last?

For anyone, the key to dissatisfaction will not be in the failure of the sincerity, but in the existence of a way to escape when things get tough. You see, the word love is used to freely that it is difficult to know what it really means. We use it to say, "1 love my wife," "l love my dog," and "1 love tacos." Obviously a man doesn't love his wife the same way he loves tacos; at least, I hope not,

The word love has a number of different meanings. Most of us look forward to falling in love because it really is a great thing. And it's something that God has designed within us. It's something truly beautiful. In order to talk about love, we need to define it. If you think you're in love right now, you need to understand what's going on inside to determine a good relationship, Could it be an illusive image? Maybe you should wait for God's timing, because He wants you to know what real love is. There are some interesting parallels in this story that God wants us to experience. In the older cultures, the father would do their choosing. In that same way, your heavenly Father wants to do the choosing also! You may have some plans, but what kind of guy would you like to marry? I've heard some interesting responses. "Well, I want him to be six feet tall, good looking with good hair, and drive a Porsche." The guy may be four feet tall, with no hair at all, and overweight! The fact is, God has chosen a certain person for you because He knows what is best for you and him. God is trying to make some changes in you. One day you will meet that special person, and you will be prepared for each other.

The parallel is God's timing. Isaac was probably in his late thirties when he married. But he was seeking the Lord rather than tearing up the landscape looking for a wife. Does that mean you should never be around girls or guys? Not at all! Get out there, guys! Look around! There's nothing wrong with that. But don't be obsessed with it. We should never make that the passion and pursuit of life. The Lord will show you the right person at the right time.

"THE CONCLUSION OF THE WHOLE MATTER"

Our charge, through the Word of God, is to go and teach the gospel and compel men to come unto Christ. We must declare this Word everywhere we go to the end of the world. Do not worry about delays or blocks to hinder you, but know that the battle is already won and victory is ours. We must declare this Word everywhere we go and to the end of the world. Do not worry about delays or blocks to hinder you, but know that the battle is already won and victory is yours!

"Productive Women of God, 'The Author;" stands in the gap with much praise and thanks to God, in allowing me to extend my love to everyone in the world! "the kingdom of heaven suffereth violence, and the violent take it by force" (Matt.11:12). Fight the war, be violent, and take back the Kingdom of God. In your victory, you will see souls saved, deliverance taken place and the captive set free. If you constantly attempt to restrain a person from going forth in their gifts they will eventually grow weary and not be effective. I say to you, establish yourself in the Lord by being grounded and rooted on a solid foundation. Build your foundation with the Word of God and build daily. It may take years, but do not stop building! Once a foundation is laid, you will be able to withstand the trials and tribulations of life.

You will be tossed to and fro, but still stand., You will be knocked down, but get back up. You will be persecuted and tried, talked about, damaged, criticized, and mistreated, but you can come forth as pure gold.The mind is a powerful tool. You hold people hostage when you harbor anger and hostility in your hearts against them because of their actions, which were not acceptable to you, or to someone you are affectionate toward. Therefore, you build this mighty stronghold as a blockade against their progress. You have set yourself up for a great fall, Satan will use your pass as a tool against you, and you will tumble down to destruction.

God has given each of us spiritual gifts for the perfecting of the ministry. No gift is greater than other gifts. We should not be envious or jealous of each other's gift, but encourage, exhort, and motivate one another without complaint. Stand strong in your faith, show love, be tenderhearted, kind, compassionate, and win back the Kingdom of God. Strengthen our daily walk in the Lord, and go forward in warfare battle against the enemy. Fight for freedom and deliverance in the lives of the people of God and run the victory race to the end. The Word of God has given you a prescription to live by, which is the Word of God. Dress yourself in the armor of the word, position yourself through the study of the word! "Let us here with the conclusion of the whole matter: Fear God, and keep his commandments: for the Kingdom of God!

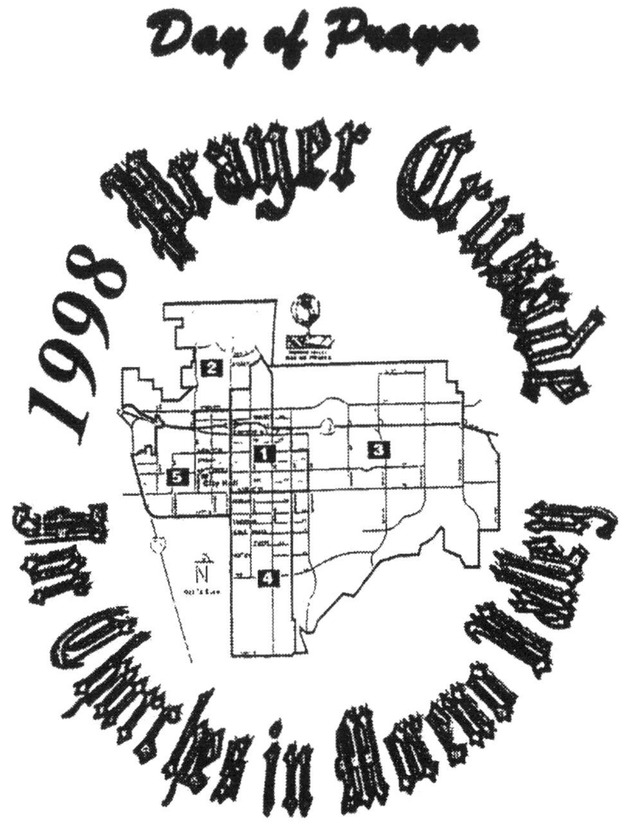

II Chronicles 7:14

Evangelist Mildred Spencer, Founder 12765 Shadybend Dr.

Moreno Valley, Ca, 92553

Email - Evangy1@aol.com

Greetings from the Founder

To all pastors churches, and well wishers. spectacular would not be too strong a word to describe what God through this servant has developed for you in your fast growing city, Moreno Valley, and surrounding areas. Our little Country place use to be called "Sunny Mead," CA, Long before the name was changed to A city called Moreno Valley CA, in the year of 1998

At that time the City of Moreno Valley's population is estimated at 135,000. Can you see the souls searching and reaching out for help? The city can't do it, but it will be done when come together declaring peace in this city and other cities.

What about this prayer crusade?

This organization was founded for the primary purpose of churches coming together praying for this nation. And praying for a spiritual awakening energizing pastors across this land for their much labor. ing. Many of them have great visions and God has entrusted them for the building up of His kingdom.

However, my mission at "age 20" was to go into all the world & preach the Gospel, act 2: 38 Peter said "Repent and be baptized in the name of Jesus Christ for forgiveness of your sins and ye shall receive the gift of the Holy Spirit, Jesus is my boss and I am his vessel! I must also carry out my commission with God's prayer Crusade.

With these churches coming together and praying, the strongholds must come down! This world is in trouble. God has given to me the burden of "help ministry", through 'prayer'. Praying for every pastor and churches everywhere. Souls are sick and need to be healed.

Therefore, I need your support! Together we can make differences. The Bibles says in Matthew 18:19, reminding you and I "that if two of you shall agree on earth as touching anything that they shall ask, it shall be done for them of my Father which is in heaven."

I guaranteed you: this is the most exciting news: intense praying resulted in the powerful proclamation of Christ. In Acts 1:14 the church is found seeking the face of God. They were with one mind continually devoting themselves to prayer, and 3,000 people were converted in this mighty visitation of God (Acts 2:441).

This should be ample evidence. The relationship between prayer and the phenomenal growth to the New Testament Church.

Questions & Answers

Who Can Participate?

Everyone! Churches of any denomination, Christians and non-Christians.

What Day and Time?

The Prayer Crusade is once a month on the last Saturday in each month. The time is from 9:00 p.m.. until midnight. Three hours of prayer, praise and thanksgiving unto our Almighty God in the name of our Lord and Savior, Jesus Christ.

Where is the Meeting Place?

The Prayer Crusades will be scheduled to convene at each church registered on a rotating basis, at a different location each month, so that each church will have an opportunity to host this great prayer event!

How Will I be Notified of the Monthly Prayer Crusade Locations?

At each meeting place, before dismissal, and announcement will be made regarding the location for the following month.

For Additional Information:

Email - Evangy1@aol.com

Thanks

Many, many thanks to all of the pastors for your commitment to this "Prayer Crusade'. So many of you have come in with such enthusiasm.

Pastor Funchess SR.
Yeshua malanatha church
Pastor Warrick

Evangelist Mildred Spencer, Founder

DIFFERENT KINDS OF PRAYER

Lord, I am moved by what I've learned today. I had no idea how much pain You endured to pay the price for my physical healing. Forgive me for the times I've tolerated sickness and didn't even pray to be healed. Now I understand that Your desire to see me healed is so great that You paid a price far beyond anything I will ever be able to comprehend. Since my physical well-being is that important to You, starting today I determine to walk in divine health and healing. I am taking a stand of faith to walk in healing and to fully possess the health You bought for me that day when You were so severely beaten!

I pray this in Jesus' name!

Lord, thank You for the blessings You have given to my family and me. You have abundantly blessed me, and I am so grateful for everything You have done. I ask You to help me keep the right attitude toward others who have less than I do; to refrain from a false attitude of pride or haughtiness; and to see myself as the manager of divinely assigned funds. I want to trust in You, Lord —- not in the things You have placed at my disposal. Possessions and material things are fleeting, but You are always the same. Therefore, I choose to fix my hope on You and not on the financial increase with which You have blessed me.

I pray this in Jesus' name!

Lord, I ask You to help me be more like Jesus! Help me release the grudges and deeply-held resentments that I am tempted to carry toward people. Instead of rejoicing when they get in trouble or when something bad happens to them, help me to reach out to them, to see what I can do to help, and to become the hand of God in their lives. Forgive me that I haven't already acted as Jesus would act, and help me learn how to put any negative emotions aside so I can reach out to them in the name of Jesus!

I pray this in Jesus' name!

Lord, thank You for being such a good example of love that is unshaken and unaffected by other people's actions. You have loved me with a consistent love, even in times when I've acted badly and didn't deserve it. Thank You so much for loving me in spite of the things I've done and the things I've permitted to go on in my life. Today I want to ask You to help me love others just as consistently as You have loved me. Forgive me for being on-again, off-again in my love. Help me become rock-solid and unwavering in my love for others, including those who haven't treated me too nicely. I know that with Your help, I can love them steadfastly no matter what they do!

I pray this in Jesus' name!

Lord, because You have given me the promises of Your Word and the right to use Your name, I refuse to let the devil bombard my mind any longer. Right now I stand up to resist him, oppose him, and put him on the run. Devil, you will no longer have free access to my mind and emotions, for I am standing up to resist you. You better put on your running shoes, because if you stick around me, I intend to prosecute you with the full authority of God's Word! I tell you to GO in Jesus' name! And, Heavenly Father, I thank You so much for giving me the great privilege of using Your Word and the authority of Jesus' name!

I pray this in Jesus' name!

First of all, Lord, I thank You for loving me enough to put people over me who were willing to bring correction into my life in the past. Although that correction was difficult to receive, I needed it and it ultimately benefited my life. For this, I am so thankful. Second, I ask You to help me now to be a blessing to those You have placed under my sphere of authority. When I see attitudes in them that need to be corrected, help me know how to approach them in a way that is positive and uplifting. I ask You to give me the wisdom I need to challenge those under my authority to a higher level in every area of their lives.

I pray this in Jesus' name!

Lord, I admit that I've been feeling pretty lonely in the situation I am facing right now. Even though my friends try to understand, they simply can't comprehend the emotional ordeal I am going through. But I know that You understand everything, Lord, so today I am asking You to step forward and assist me in my hour of need. Please stand at my side to help me, support me, and fill me with afresh dose of the Holy Spirit's mighty power so I can victoriously overcome in the midst of this challenging trial. I know that with Your Presence and power at my side, I will win this fight of faith that I am engaged in right now.

I pray this in Jesus' name!

Lord, I am so glad You have the power to put an end to my problems! So many times I've acted just like Peter, I was in the strength of my own flesh as I've tried to solve my problems without Your help. Forgive me for wasting so much time and energy! Today I ask You to speak to my heart and tell me what I am supposed to do; then help me follow Your instructions to the letter. Give me the patience to wait while You supernaturally work behind the scenes to resolve my questions.

I pray this in Jesus' name!

Lord, I ask You to help me see exactly where I should sow my finances. Please help me to see those people and organizations that will wisely handle the money I sow; then give me the ability to sow into those places with elation and joy! I want to be excited about my giving! I want to give, knowing that my gift is truly going to make a huge difference. And as I give to benefit others, I ask You to honor Your Word and multiply it back to me again so I can continue to give and be a blessing to the Christian community.

I pray this in Jesus' name!

1. How often do you reflect on the work of Christ on the Cross?
2. Have you ever taken time to think of what it must have been like for Jesus to take the sins of the whole world upon Himself?
3. How would it affect you if you read each Gospel's account of the crucifixion over and over again for an entire month? Why don't you commit to doing this and see what God does in your heart as you read, reread, and meditate on these Important scriptures?

HEALING SCRIPTURES

Proverbs 4:20: My son, attend to my words; incline thine ear unto my sayings (KJV).

Proverbs 4:21: Let them not depart from thine eyes; keep them in the midst of thine heart (KJV).

Proverbs 4:22: For they are life unto those that find them, and health to all their flesh (KJV).

Isaiah 53:4: Surely he hath borne our griefs, and carried our sorrows: yet we did esteem him stricken, smitten of God, and afflicted (KJV).

Isaiah 53:5: But he was wounded for our transgressions, he was bruised for our iniquities: the chastisement of our peace was upon him; and with his stripes we are healed (KJV).

Matthew 4:23: And Jesus went about all Galilee, teaching in their synagogues, and preaching the gospel of the kingdom, and healing all manner of sickness and all manner of disease among the people (KJV).

Mark 5:38-39: And he cometh to the house of the ruler of the synagogue, and seeth the tumult, and them that wept and wailed greatly, and when he was come in, he said unto them. Why make ye this ado, and weep? the damsel is not dead, but sleepeth (KJV).

Printed in the United States
By Bookmasters